RECRUITMENT, SELECTION, AND RETENTION OF LAW ENFORCEMENT OFFICERS

Patrick Oliver

Foreword by Sylvester Daughtry, Jr.

**This publication is dedicated to the hard-working
law enforcement officers who risk their lives
every day to protect and serve the community.**

www.blue360media.com

To contact Blue360° Media, LLC, please call: **1-844-599-2887**

ISBN: 978-1-932777-96-3

Blue360° Media, LLC
2750 Rasmussen Rd., Suite 107
Park City, Utah 84098
1-844-599-2887
www.blue360media.com

(Pub. 93014)

TABLE OF CONTENTS

Dedication

This book is dedicated to the following individuals who represent my immediate family support system in this life.

My wife, Kim
My daughter, Brittney
My sons, Jason & Justin
My father, James, Sr.
My mother, Mary
My two brothers, James and Michael
My in-laws, John and Emmy Lou Miller

Acknowledgments

I would like to acknowledge and express my sincere appreciation to the following people and organizations who have helped me, each in their own way, to complete this book:

My wife, Kim Oliver, whose patience, love, and support has been invaluable to me. To my daughter, Brittney, who is truly my loving princess. To my sons, Jason and Justin, who keep me young and teach me how to have fun. To my dad, James W. Oliver, Sr., who modeled a love of law enforcement for me. To my mom, Mary Jane Oliver, who always has wise counsel.

I want to thank Sylvester Daughtry, Jr., for writing the Foreword and the Commission on Accreditation for Law Enforcement Agencies for allowing me to reprint two chapters of the Standards Manual in this book for the furtherance of the law enforcement profession. To the International Association of Chiefs of Police for sharing its organizational knowledge and established professional practices. To the Ohio State Highway Patrol for providing me with my initial law enforcement training and providing information beneficial to writing this book. Finally, to the Columbus Division of Police for its willingness to share documents to enhance material in this book.

About the Author

Patrick Oliver is currently Director of the Criminal Justice Program for Cedarville University and recently served as Chief of Police for the City of Fairborn, Ohio. He previously served as Chief of Police in Grandview Heights, Cleveland, Ohio, and the Ranger Chief of Cleveland Metropolitan Park District. Other law enforcement experience includes 11 years as a trooper with the Ohio State Highway Patrol.

He is a 1989 graduate of Penn State University Police Executive School, a graduate of the FBI's Law Enforcement Executive Development School in 1993, and a graduate of the Ohio Association Chiefs of Police Executive Leadership College in 1994. He became a Certified Law Enforcement Executive (CLEE) in 1996. He is also a graduate of the rural Executive Management Institute. Oliver holds a Bachelor of Arts Degree in Criminal Justice and a Masters Degree in Business Administration, both from Baldwin Wallace College, Berea, Ohio. He also has a Ph.D. in Leadership and Change from Antioch University, Yellow Springs, Ohio.

Chief Oliver has previously taught Criminal Justice and business courses at Cuyahoga Community College, and Wright State University. He serves as a consultant and a trainer with the Ohio Association of Chiefs of Police, the International Association of Chiefs of Police, and the National Organization of Black Law Enforcement Executives. He is also a past commissioner for the Commission of Accreditation for Law Enforcement Agencies. He is a Past President for the Ohio Association of Chiefs of Police. He is a member of the Civil Rights committee for International Association of Chiefs of Police and the Director of the Chief Executive Officers Mentoring Program for the National Organization of Black Law Enforcement Executives.

Foreword

The recruitment, selection, and retention of law enforcement officers are among the greatest challenges facing the Chief Executive Officer of a law enforcement agency today. The competition for qualified candidates is fierce and is further intensified given the many options the desired candidate has when choosing a type of agency for employment.

Patrick Oliver, a former chief of police and past commissioner with the Commission on Accreditation for Law Enforcement Agencies, now directs the Criminal Justice Program at Cedarville University as well as conducts a mentoring program for the National Organization of Black Law Enforcement Executives. He has conducted extensive research on the recruitment of law enforcement officers and is now sharing his knowledge of this critically important responsibility. This information should prove to be a tremendous resource for the twenty-first century law enforcement Chief Executive Officer.

Sylvester Daughtry, Jr.
Executive Director
Commission on Accreditation for Law Enforcement Agencies Inc.
(CALEA®)

Why I Wrote This Book

During the mid-1990s, while serving as a Police Chief, I personally became frustrated by the media accounts of law enforcement officers being disciplined, suspended, and terminated for unethical or illegal behavior. There were also media reports of law enforcement officers being indicted and/or convicted of criminal behavior. It is always disturbing when law enforcement officers are involved in criminal or unethical behavior on or off the job. It made me wonder how all of these individuals got hired as law enforcement officers. Other relevant questions are: Do law enforcement agencies hire bad officers or do they make bad officers? Are officers hired that agencies know, or should have known, are unfit for the job? Does the law enforcement agency culture contribute to misconduct? Law enforcement agencies sometimes maintain an environment and culture which encourage officers to behave badly. How should the law enforcement profession respond to this serious assault on its integrity? More importantly, what are the knowledge, skills, and traits that are predictive of effectiveness in the law enforcement officer job? These questions were ones, I believed, worthy of research.

Therefore, in 1998, I applied for a grant with the Ohio Office of Criminal Justice Services to study the hiring of law enforcement officers. Approval of the grant was given to do a pilot study of five Ohio law enforcement agencies to evaluate the process and potential effectiveness of the hiring process for law enforcement officers. The five law enforcement agencies selected were of different sizes and types. The following Ohio law enforcement agencies participated in this study: Ohio State Highway Patrol; Columbus Division of Police; The Ohio State University Police Department; Montgomery County Sheriff's Department; and the Zanesville Police Department. The diversity of agencies was for the purpose of making recommendations regarding the selection of law enforcement officers that could apply to all law enforcement agencies in the United States. The primary purpose of this research grant is to help law enforcement administrators identify desirable behaviors and traits in law enforcement candidates. A key methodology used was the Entry-Level Assessment Center method, which focused on both identifying and evaluating successful job-related behaviors and traits. I believed that a law enforcement agency should determine the agency-specific successful law enforcement officer behaviors and traits first, and then design a selection process to identify these candidates. This two-step method is a great way to improve hiring quality. The Entry-Level Assessment Center is only one recommended component of the selection process and should be used to complement the other selection components.

As the law enforcement profession continues to face contemporary issues, all administrators face the same challenge, which is meeting the demand for entry-level leadership talent. Leadership talent hired at the entry level should be retained and developed at every level of the organization. Does your law enforcement agency need to worry about organizational talent? Here are some questions to consider:

- Will your agency have the leadership bench strength to staff its growth or development plans?
- Have you hired entry-level leaders to lead the agency in the future?
- If the people in your agency are not competitive professionally, how can your agency be competitive in the profession?
- Has the agency had to compromise on leadership quality to fill entry-level positions?
- Have your law enforcement roles and challenges changed significantly over the past five to ten years?
- What percentage of current officers would be hired if they were applying today?
- Have you identified the knowledge, skills, abilities, education, experience, behaviors, and traits your agency desires for law enforcement officers?

If your answers to these questions leave you feeling a bit uneasy, or if you do not have the answers, it might be time to make the search for leadership a priority in your agency. This book was written and designed to help law enforcement leaders with their single most important managerial tasks, which is the recruitment, selection, and retention of effective law enforcement officers. My passion to help law enforcement agencies get answers to these questions began this journey, which continues still today.

How Might You Benefit By Reading This Book

Law enforcement agencies have worked hard to find viable ways of recruiting, selecting, and retaining law enforcement officers. Most agencies will publicly advertise the position and use a multi-step hiring process that consists of six to twelve steps. Retention typically is a result of how the agency is managed without much planning and preparation of how to retain quality officers. One of the great issues of our time in the profession of law enforcement is how to effectively recruit, select, and retain law enforcement officers.

The recruitment, selection, and retention of high-quality law enforcement officers are key issues of the law enforcement profession today. In reality, these always been important issues; however, today, quality candidates have been more difficult to find by many law enforcement agencies across America. Hiring employees, and of course law enforcement officers, is the single most important managerial task. This is because the quality of an organization is reduced to the quality of the employee with whom the customer is dealing. A law enforcement organization could be the worst in a given area, but if the officer treats a community member with care and compassion, from the citizen's perspective, this agency is excellent. Conversely, a law enforcement agency could be the best in an area, but if the officer treats the community member disrespectfully, then as far as he or she is concerned, it is a poor agency. It seems that every law enforcement manager claims that its people are the most important resource. If this is true, the process for identifying and selecting candidates should reflect this. Proper planning, sufficient time, and financial resources should be allocated to this most critical management function.

It is very sobering, but I have come to realize the two most effective decisions any manager can make. The first is hiring an effective employee. The reason for this is simple: Quality products or services are provided primarily by quality people. If the people in your organization are not competitive in the profession, how could the organization be competitive in the profession? Quality products and services are always obstructed by the ability to hire top talent. The second most effective decision any manager can make is to terminate an ineffective employee. Even though this may sound unkind, in reality it is not. People should have the ability to be successful at what they do every day. This can occur only if people are placed in jobs that match their talents and abilities. All hiring, special assignments, and promotions should match the talents and abilities of the individual. When a person is placed in a job that matches his or her talents and abilities, it is good for the customers, the organization, and the individual. When they are not, it is bad for all three.

A key function of law enforcement recruitment and selection processes has been to screen for candidate deficiencies that might result in job failure. The selection processes in particular are largely effective in accomplishing this goal in that they usually detect severe and obvious candidate behavior deficiencies. However, eliminating candidates who demonstrate behavioral deficiencies does not necessarily mean that those candidates who remain will have the skills necessary for job success. Finding candidates who possess the desired characteristics is a proactive process that must be purposely structured into the recruitment and selection process. Once these high-performing individuals have been recruited and selected then effective strategies must be used to retain them.

This book is designed to be both a how-to manual and idea guide for law enforcement administrators and other government officials involved in the process of the recruitment, selection, or retention of law enforcement officers. It contains a collection of standards in the law enforcement profession, legal mandates, best practices, and recommendations based on criminal justice research. These strategies should be compared and contrasted with an agency's current operation to determine which are the most viable based on economic, political, legal, and operational considerations. Therefore, these strategies may or may not be usable exactly as recommended. It is up to the agency to modify these strategies as appropriate.

How to Use this Book

Fundamentally, this book may be used by any individuals involved in the recruitment, selection, and retention of law enforcement officers in one of two ways. First, an administrator might use this book to modify their entire hiring process. They may believe that their hiring process needs to be revised completely. This book is designed to assist an agency in doing just that. Take the best ideas that fit your agency and use them; eliminate the parts that are not applicable to your job environment. Of course, all applicable legal mandates and human resource laws must be followed that affect the hiring process. Second, an individual or administrator may use this book to revise one or several components of the hiring process. If there are only one or two components that you are interested in revising, you can refer to those particular chapters. In either case this book is designed to guide you on why and how to more effectively recruit, select, and retain law enforcement officers.

At the end of each chapter written on the process of recruitment, selection, and retention of law enforcement officers, there is a list of recommendations. These bulleted recommendations provide a quick easy-to-read overview of the key information that is provided in that chapter. This ensures that main points of each chapter are clearly understood. Hopefully, you will find this book interesting, informative, and thought provoking as you evaluate your agency's process for recruiting, selecting, and retaining law enforcement officers.

Chapter 1

Selection Criteria for Law Enforcement Officers

Why Hiring is Critical

In the twenty-first century, law enforcement agencies face the great challenge of hiring the contemporary law enforcement officers in a market that appears to have a diminishing number of qualified candidates.

- What knowledge, skills, abilities, behavior, and traits should agencies seek?
- How do we determine what these qualities are?
- Have our needs changed?
- Is the candidate pool changing?
- How do we effectively develop and implement a recruitment plan?
- How do we structure our selection process and why?
- What are the key issues in law enforcement officer retention?

The hiring of a law enforcement officer is the single most important function of any law enforcement agency. The officers hired provide the service to our community members. The quality of all law enforcement service is reduced to the officer(s) our community member(s) are dealing with. No amount of organization or equipment will replace the human relation skills of the individual officer. Selecting the best candidates in the marketplace is paramount. It is primarily the officers hired at entry level that become the future managers for an agency. The quality of the individuals you hire will determine the quality of the organization. If the officers in your organization are not competitive in the law enforcement profession, how can your organization be competitive in the law enforcement profession? The single most important task of a law enforcement chief executive officer (CEO) is hiring people. Therefore, the CEO should be directly involved in the hiring process and treat it as a priority. Whoever controls the hiring process controls the effectiveness of the law enforcement agency. If CEOs are too busy to become involved in the hiring process, then they are just too busy.

It is the people who obtain the results and accomplish the mission of any agency. People are the most important resource in any organization. This fact is acknowledged by everyone, is not denied by anyone, written about by many, but practiced by very few agencies.

Successful Law Enforcement Officer Traits

Most law enforcement agencies have a multi-step hiring process that contains between six to twelve components from a written exam to a pre-employment physical examination. The components of the hiring process in many agencies have not changed in decades, even though the type of officer desired has changed. The first step in identifying the selection criteria for the law enforcement officers at your agency is to identify essential job functions, successful job-related behaviors and traits. In 1999 I was awarded a grant as the project director to conduct a study on the hiring of law enforcement officers within the State of Ohio. Approval of the grant was given to do a pilot study of five Ohio law enforcement agencies to evaluate the process and potential effectiveness of the hiring process for law enforcement officers. The five law enforcement agencies selected were of different sizes and types.

The following Ohio law enforcement agencies participated in this study: Ohio State Highway Patrol; Columbus Division of Police; The Ohio State University Police Department; Montgomery County Sheriff's Department; and the Zanesville Police Department. The diversity of agencies was for the purpose of making recommendations regarding the selection of law enforcement officers, which could apply to all law enforcement agencies in the United States. The 1999 – 2000 Ohio Law Enforcement Foundation Research Study grant for hiring law enforcement officers identified 12 common traits desired by law enforcement agencies regardless of agency size or type. Job analysis survey instruments used at five different Ohio law enforcement agencies indicated that these traits are desirable to varying degrees for all of these agencies.

The Ohio Law Enforcement Research Study indicated that the following traits are desirable for law enforcement officers. These traits are viewed to be foundational, and therefore, in your selection criteria it is recommended that these knowledge, skills, abilities, behaviors, and traits be considered for validation:

Integrity: The candidate has high moral and ethical standards and possesses integrity in all matters, public, and private.

Human Diversity Skills: The candidate has the ability to act in an unbiased manner and must have an understanding of human diversity issues demonstrating cultural competency.

Service Orientation: The candidate has a service orientation: a desire and commitment to service above self.

Team Compatibility: The candidate has a team orientation. The candidate has the ability to work with others in a cooperative, caring, and supportive manner to achieve goals of the group.

Oral Communication Skill: The candidate has the ability to communicate well orally. The candidate is a good listener and can clearly transmit thoughts and ideas to others.

Written Communication Skill: The candidate has the ability to communicate well in writing and the ability to convey an idea, concept, or information in a clear, concise, and appropriate format.

Motivation: The candidate has the ability to be highly motivated while working independently.

Decision-Making: The candidate has the ability to be a good decision maker and problem solver.

Human Relations Skill: The candidate has the ability to interact with people, effectively demonstrating good human relation skills.

Self-Control: The candidate has the ability to maintain self-control under stressful circumstances. Self-discipline is critical to responding properly.

Planning and Organizing Skill: The candidate has planning and organizing skills.

Performance Driven: The candidate is performance driven and has the desire and motivation to be successful in achieving group and individual goals.

The Five Most Important Traits

After completing this law enforcement hiring study in 2000, I had the opportunity of presenting the findings approximately 20 times over the next four years to about 2,000 law enforcement officers from the United States and Canada. These groups contained officers from local, state, and federal law enforcement agencies. In those presentations of the study, there was never an occasion in which any law enforcement official or administrator ever indicated (after being asked) that any one of these twelve traits did not apply to law enforcement officers at their agency. This is not to suggest that these traits should not be validated through a job task analysis. It is only to suggest that they are highly recommended to be considered for evaluating in a law enforcement job. Of these twelve traits there are five that are the most important. They all have value but I suggest these five are the most essential to screen for in a law enforcement officer job. When selecting for a law enforcement officer you are hiring an entry-level leader. If I was to summarize what all law enforcement agencies are looking for in one word, it is "leadership." I certainly understand that this is an overused word that has been highly researched and written about. However, it does provide the essence of what law enforcement agencies are looking for. I believe it also describes what the "military academies" and "Ivy league" schools are also seeking in their students. Here they are in what I would consider their order of importance.

It should be no surprise that **Integrity** is the most important. An American peace officer has more power and authority than any other job I can think of in our society. A peace officer can issue a verbal warning, a written warning, a citation (which is a summons to appear in court at a later time), make an arrest, make an arrest with force, can make an arrest with deadly force. Each one of these acts of law enforcement intervention may be deemed legal. A mayor, judge, congressman, or the president of the United States cannot do this. With this tremendous amount of authority comes the responsibility to be a man or woman of high moral character. The peace officer wears the badge of trust, which is a privilege and not a right, reserved only for those who serve with honor.

Second is the trait of **Service**. Service is what is sold in the profession of law enforcement. Approximately 80 percent of the job is service and 20 percent of it is enforcement. This is true at a major city P.D. or a small town P.D. Community service is what is being most provided to residents, businesses, and visitors of the community. Helping, assisting, and guiding hurt people is a skill that is invaluable in a profession that operates 24 hours a day, as the most visible part of government. It is truly a helping profession.

Third is the trait of effective **Human Relations Skills**. The job of a law enforcement officer is meeting and dealing with people. A law enforcement officer is someone who has to go into a negative situation and attempt to leave people with something positive. If this is done properly then one leaves people better than they found them. If a person gets tired of people, or is easily frustrated with people, or is not caring and compassionate, he or she is not suited for law enforcement. There are many times law enforcement officers are dealing with people at their worst. It takes great human relations skills to manage conflict or problems in a patient, caring, and professional manner.

Fourth is the trait of **Team Compatibility**. Law enforcement agencies operate on the concept of team. This requires that the goals of the individual are subordinate to the goals of the team or organization. A peace officer must come in early, stay late, be on call, work weekends, evenings, nights, and holidays. This takes a team player who understands that a law enforcement agency is a service profession operating 24 hours a day for the benefit of the community. This person also understands that by accepting employment they agreed to do whatever needs to be done as long as it is legal or ethical with a positive mental attitude. They have made an individual commitment to the organization's success.

Fifth is the trait of being **Performance Driven**. Law enforcement officers generally work independently. It is a job that requires people who want to be the best they can be. The only real competition they face is being their best. They are involved daily in self-initiated activity. These individuals are serving the community other than the times when they get a call for service. They set and achieve individual and professional goals to become better tomorrow than they were yesterday. They are contributors to the organization's standard of excellence.

The Value of Emotional Intelligence

You might summarize these five key traits as being "character centered." A law enforcement agency should do character-based hiring. The United States Community Oriented Policing Service several years ago labeled this philosophy as hiring in the "spirit of service." This federally funded project recommended that each agency prior to hiring identify a common core of "service-oriented" traits because the job emphasizes service more than enforcement (Scrivner, 2004). These five traits are indicative of an officer's emotional intelligence (EQ) versus their intelligence quotient (IQ). There has been much written about emotional intelligence over the last several decades. Emotional Intelligence is defined as the intelligent management of your emotions (Goleman, Boyatzis, & McKee, 1999). Policing, more than other professions, demands that officers bring intelligent emotions to bear, especially when responding to calls for service involving conflict among people. It is helpful to understand that for all jobs that exist in the world EQ is more important than IQ (Goleman, 1995). Individuals hired in law enforcement should have the mental horsepower to do the job. However, beyond having the required level of intelligence (IQ), it is one's emotional intelligence that mostly contributes to job effectiveness.

Goleman indicated (1995) it is well known in psychology that grades, IQ or SAT scores, despite their popular mystique, do not predict unerringly who will succeed in life. At best it is estimated that IQ contributes about 20% to the factors that determine success in life, which leaves 80% to other forces. The ability to excel academically does not indicate how one reacts to the vicissitudes of life.

There are four domains that together constitute emotional intelligence. The first two are self-awareness and self-management, which are skills reflective of the individuals (personal competence). Self-awareness is your ability to perceive your emotions in the moment and effectively understand them across situations. Self-management is your ability to use your awareness to stay flexible to respond with positive behaviors to people and situations. The other two domains are social awareness and relationship management, which indicate how you relate to other people (social competence). Social awareness is your ability to discern the emotions of other people to effectively understand their perspective. Relationship management is the use of the first three emotional intelligence skills to manage human interactions effectively. To expand on this understanding, intelligence quotient (IQ) and emotional intelligence (EQ) and personality are three distinct qualities we all possess. Intelligence is your ability to learn, and does not change throughout your life (not flexible). Emotional intelligence is a flexible skill that is learnable. There is no connection between EQ and IQ. It is not possible to predict one based on the other. An individual may be intelligent but not emotionally intelligent, and people of all types of personalities can be high in EQ and/or IQ. Personality is the style that defines you. It is based on your preferences such as an inclination toward extroversion or introversion. Of these three, emotional intelligence is the only attribute that is flexible and changeable (Bradberry & Greaves 2005). I like to think of it this way; it's not how smart you are it's how you are smart. In the service-oriented profession of law enforcement, requiring men and women of character, agencies need to focus on the qualities that produce job related effectiveness. How do you evaluate a law enforcement candidate for these qualities? You must screen for them in several of the components of the selection process. Chapter 12 on oral interviews discusses how to do behavioral-based interviewing to select for these qualities.

Evaluating the Law Enforcement Officer Job at Your Agency

The 12 traits represent a comprehensive list of qualities desired for all law enforcement officers. The list of qualities your agency requires may include additional traits. To determine what these additional traits are requires conducting a job analysis for the entry-level law enforcement officer. This job analysis entails reviewing, at a minimum, the following information at your agency: the mission statement; core values of the agency; agency goals; job description for a law enforcement officer; community needs survey information; interviews and/or focus groups with individuals in the target job; interviews and/or focus groups with individuals who manage and oversee the target job (all levels of management are ideal), as well as community members and reviewing any previous job task analysis information if available. The addition of this information helps evaluate the list of traits and qualities desirable for law enforcement officers in your agency. Chapter 2 on Job Task Analysis provides some fundamental guidelines on this critical step of defining the job.

The qualities desired for law enforcement officers today have certainly changed. If you doubt this, then ask yourself if the job of law enforcement officers has changed in the last ten years in your community. Will the job probably be different in the future? I believe the answer to both of these questions is "yes." The important question is: Has the criteria your agency utilizes for selecting a law enforcement officer changed? The starting place is to determine what the knowledge, skills, abilities, education, behaviors, and traits are desired for someone who effectively performs the job.

The development of a flexible profile of a contemporary law enforcement officer is critical to designing the recruitment and selection process.

Is the Candidate Pool Changing?

Is the candidate pool changing for law enforcement candidates? (Cole, Smith, & Lucas, 2002) I believe the answer is a resounding, yes! In research done by Arkansas Tech University, authors Cole, Smith & Lucas indicate certain characteristics among younger generations. There is an observable shift in many new generation law enforcement candidates. While there are some exceptions, some of these debatable changes include the following:

- Work is not a big part of their lives.
- Focus on lifestyle first, then work to support it.
- Less family stability.
- Want to have a direct "say" in how their work is done.
- General lack of a military background.
- They have a more global outlook, and
- Less flexibility to administrative requirements.

Candidates seem to have:

- More education — *Are they more intelligent?*
- Greater appreciation of diversity.
- More access to physical training equipment and expertise — *Are they in better or worse physical condition?*

- More technological abilities.
- More career options.

The change in the candidate pool of qualified law enforcement applicants dictates that law enforcement agencies evaluate and modify their methods of recruitment and selection of candidates on a periodic basis.

The chart that follows compares and contrasts the value of knowledge, skills, and abilities (KSAs), (generally IQ) and personal behaviors and traits (EQ). In the profession of law enforcement when officers are disciplined, suspended, or terminated is it because of a lack of technical abilities or skills, or is it because of negative behaviors or traits displayed on or off the job? The vast majority of times job actions are based on negative behaviors and traits. Because this is the case, why don't we screen and select for positive behaviors and traits? It is important to both eliminate candidates unsuitable for the job and identify candidates most suitable for the job. As you study this chart to comprehend its message, please note that the ability to do KSAs does not equal the desire to do. Just because someone has certain technical skills and abilities does not mean they are willing to use them effectively for the benefit of an organization.

Knowledge, Skills, & Abilities and Behaviors & Traits

KNOWLEDGE, SKILLS, & ABILITIES [ability to do]	VS.	BEHAVIORS & TRAITS [desire to do]
Easier to teach or train		Difficult or impossible to teach or train
Acquired post-hire		Acquired pre-hire
By itself, leads to moderate performance at best		Plus KSAs will take an individual from moderate to excellent performance
Causes few disciplinary problems		Causes most of the disciplinary problems
Results in few employment terminations		Results in most employment terminations
Over-emphasized in its value in the selection process of job candidates		Under-emphasized in its value in the selection process of job candidates
Based on research contributes at most 20 percent to job performance		Based on research contributes approximately 80 percent to job performance

In their book, *The Emotional Intelligence Quick Book*, the authors Bradberry and Greaves, indicate that the concept of emotional intelligence can explained why two people of the same IQ can attain vastly different levels so success in life. You cannot predict emotional intelligence based on how smart someone is, this is good news because cognitive intelligence or IQ, is not flexible. Intelligence is your ability to learn, and it's the same at age ten as it is at age 60. Emotional intelligence conversely is a flexible skill that is learnable.

"Consistent with the principles of emotional intelligence, behaviors and traits, which are indicative of emotional intelligence (EQ), are more important for the entry level law enforcement job than knowledge, skills, and abilities, which are indicative of intelligence quotient (IQ)."   — Patrick Oliver

Recommendations and Key Points for Law Enforcement Officer Selection Criteria

- The market for law enforcement officers appears to have a diminishing number of qualified candidates.
- The hiring of a law enforcement officer is the single most important function of any law enforcement agency.
- The quality of service provided in law enforcement is reduced to the quality of the officers.
- The chief executive officer of a law enforcement agency must give priority to the task of hiring.
- The Ohio Law Enforcement Foundation Research Study identified 12 traits desired by law enforcement agencies regardless of agency size or type.
- There are five of the 12 traits that are the most important qualities to screen for, of which integrity is the most important.
- It is recommended that a law enforcement agency do "character-based hiring."
- One's intelligence quotient and emotional intelligence both contribute to job performance. However, for all jobs EQ is more important than IQ for determining job performance.
- IQ is fixed and unchangeable, while EQ is learnable and changeable.

- To determine the attributes desired for a law enforcement officer at a specific agency, a job task analysis must be conducted.
- The change in the applicant pool dictates that law enforcement agencies evaluate and modify their methods of recruitment and selection on a periodic basis.
- The ability to perform effectively in a job does not equal the desire to be effective in a job.

References

Bradberry, T., & Greaves, J. (2005). *The emotional intelligence quick book: everything you need to know to put your EQ to work.* New York: Simon & Schuster, Inc.

Cole, G., Smith, R., & Lucas, L. (2002). *The debut of generation Y in the American workforce. Journal of Business Administration Online.* Vol. 1 No. 2.

Coleman, D. (1997). *Emotional intelligence: Why it can matter more than IQ.* New York: Bantam Books.

Goleman, Boyatzis, and McKee (2002). *Primal leadership: Realizing the power of emotional Intelligence.* Boston: Harvard Business School Press.

Scrivner, E. (2004). *Innovations in police recruitment and hiring: Hiring in the spirit of service.* U.S. Department of Justice. Office of Community Oriented Policing Services.

Chapter 2

Job Task Analysis

A Basic Human Resource Management Tool

A job consists of a group of tasks that must be performed for an organization to achieve its goals. A job may require the services of one person, such as that of Chief of Police, or the services of 75 police officers, as might be the case with a law enforcement agency. In a law enforcement work group consisting of a supervisor, seven law enforcement officers, and administrative assistant, there are three jobs and nine positions. A position is the collection of tasks and responsibilities performed by one person within a job classification. There is a position for every individual in an organization. For instance, a small law enforcement agency might have 12 jobs for its 75 employees, whereas in a large law enforcement agency, 50 jobs may exist for 2,000 employees. Job descriptions are lists of general tasks or functions and responsibilities of a position. Typically, they also include to whom the position reports, specifications such as the qualifications needed by the person on the job, salary range for the position, and so on. Job descriptions are usually developed by conducting a job analysis.

A job task analysis is the systematic process of determining the skills, duties, and knowledge required for performing jobs in an organization. It is an essential and pervasive human resource technique.

The purpose of job analysis is to obtain answers to six important questions:

1. What physical and mental tasks does the worker accomplish?
2. When is the job to be completed?
3. Where is the job to be accomplished?
4. How does the worker do the job?
5. Why is the job done?
6. What qualifications are needed to perform the job?

A job task analysis provides a summary of a job's duties, tasks, and responsibilities, its relationship to other jobs, the knowledge and skills required, and working conditions under which it is performed. Job facts are gathered, analyzed, and recorded as the job exists, not as the job should exist. The identification of new job tasks is most often assigned to industrial engineers, methods analysts, or others.

A job task analysis is performed on three occasions. First, it is done when the organization is founded, and a job analysis program is initiated for the first time. Second, it is performed when new jobs are created. Third, it is used when jobs are changed significantly as a result of new technologies, methods, procedures, or systems. Job analysis is mostly performed because of changes in the nature of jobs. Job analysis information is used to prepare both job descriptions and job postings for law enforcement jobs.

The job description is a document that provides information regarding the tasks, duties, and responsibilities of the job, as mentioned before. The minimum acceptable qualifications a person should possess to perform a particular job are contained in the job posting.

Job Task Analysis Professional Standard
(Standards for Law Enforcement Agencies, 2006, Revised)

The Commission on Accreditation for Law Enforcement Agencies (CALEA) has promulgated a law enforcement standard on conducting job task analysis. This standard requires that every full-time employee in the agency (both officers and civilians) have a written job task analysis that has been conducted and maintained on file. CALEA requires that the job task analysis contains three components. First, the job duties, responsibilities, functions, and tasks need to be indicated. Second, the frequency in which these work behaviors occur must be measured. Third, the task analysis must indicate how critical the job-related skills, knowledge, and abilities are to effectiveness in the job.

The following diagram helps to indicate the importance of a job task analysis. In the human resource profession, it is considered to be the most basic human resource management tool. A job task analysis allows an organization to identify the essential functions of a job. Essential job functions are critical to the Americans with Disabilities Act (ADA). ADA prohibits discrimination against a qualified individual with a disability. The qualified individual with a disability must be able to perform the essential functions of a job with or without reasonable accommodation. Therefore, every job description must identify essential job functions. After identifying the essential functions of a job, other job tasks may be identified based on frequency and criticality. After a job description is established, an agency can create job goals. These job goals are in alignment with the identified essential functions of the job and job tasks. A job description along with job goals creates the environment for effective job supervision. The individual supervising the job can then properly evaluate positive or negative job performance behaviors. Finally, if the supervisor is able to evaluate positive and negative job behaviors, he or she can do an effective job evaluation. From this description, it is apparent that the essential functions of the job, job description, job goals, job supervision, and job evaluation are all dependent on conducting an appropriate job task analysis.

Appendix 1 shows the inter-relationship between the job task analysis and related components of the job. Appendix 2 provides some tips on conducting a job task analysis.

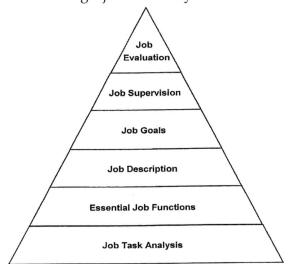

The Foundational Importance of a Job Task Analysis

Appendix 2-1
Job Analysis: The Most Basic Human
Resource Management Tool

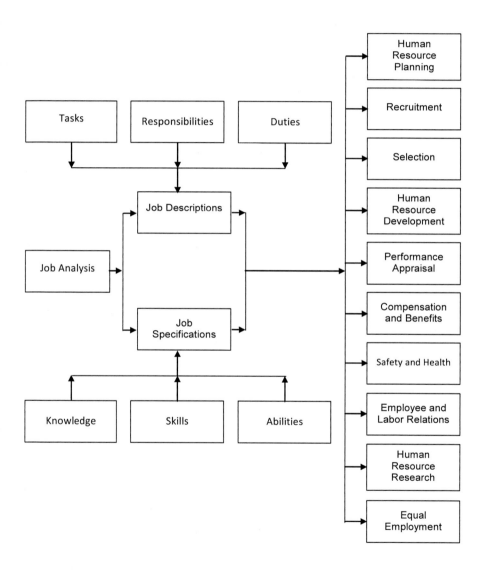

Appendix 2-2
Methods for Gathering Job Analysis Data

Job analysis data may be gathered using one of four methods:

1. Interviews with job incumbents;
2. Direct observation of the worker performing job task;
3. The use of a questionnaire with job incumbents and supervisors; or
4. Participant logs.

1. Interviews with Job Incumbents

Job incumbents are interviewed to determine "who, what, where, when, and why" they perform job task. After the job tasks are established, the interview should be structured to discussing one job task at a time. Each job task should be evaluated in regard to its frequency and importance in relation to the effectiveness in the job.

2. Direct Observation of the Worker Performing Job Task

The worker should be observed on the job performing a complete work cycle before asking any questions. Notes are taken of all the job activities observed including those not fully understood. After accumulating as much job information as possible and having a discussion to clarify things not understood, it should be determined what the worker does in addition to what has been seen.

3. The Use of a Questionnaire with Job Incumbents and Supervisors

The questionnaire is a document that asks for certain identifying information. It allows employees to describe job tasks in their own words. Establish a list of job tasks and ask the employees to rate and rank each of the job tasks by both importance and frequency. Employees are allowed to make comments concerning job tasks or to describe any job task not identified.

4. Participant Logs

This is a data-gathering methodology that requires employees to maintain a daily log or a list of things they do during the work day. As participants change from one task to another, they record the task along with the time spent on each task. Each task is rated based on importance and frequency. If the task of a job varies over a period of days, weeks, or months, job incumbents may be asked to complete logs for a specified period of time.

Recommendation and Key Points for Conducting a Job Task Analysis

- A job consists of a group of tasks that must be performed for an organization to achieve its goals.
- A position is the collection of tasks and responsibilities performed by one person within a job classification.
- A job task analysis is the systematic process of determining the skills, duties, and knowledge required for performing jobs in an organization.
- The purpose of the job task analysis is to answer six important questions.
- A job task analysis is performed on three occasions:
  - *First,* when the organization is founded.
  - *Second,* when new jobs are created.
  - *Third,* when jobs are changed significantly.
- The job description is a document that provides information regarding the task, duties, and responsibilities of the job.
- The minimum acceptable qualifications a person should possess in order to perform a particular job are contained in the job posting.
- A job task analysis helps identify the essential functions of a job.
- The Americans with Disabilities Act requires that essential job functions must be identified for every job.
- The law enforcement job task analysis must identify job tasks based on frequency and criticality.
- The foundational importance of a job task analysis is that it helps create other related components of the job.

References

Commission on Accreditation for Law Enforcement Agencies [CALEA].

Americans with Disabilities Act – signed into law July 26, 2990

Chapter 3

Advertising the Law Enforcement Job

Branding Your Law Enforcement Agency

The American Marketing Association (AMA) defines a brand as a "name, term sign, symbol or design, or a combination of them intended to identify the goods and services of one seller or group of sellers and to differentiate them from those of other sellers." An important aspect to consider is "branding." Branding for law enforcement is a method of identifying the style and manner in which your agency does policing.

The objectives of a good brand for a law enforcement agency includes:

- a clearly delivered message concerning an agency's policing philosophy;
- a confirmation of your credibility;
- an emotional connection to your service population;
- motivation for community members to become involved with the agency; and
- an incentive for community members to help prevent, reduce, and solve crime.

A brand is a symbolic embodiment of all the information connected to the product and serves to create associations and expectations around it. A brand often includes a logo, fonts, color schemes, and sound, which may be developed to represent implicit values, ideas, and even organizational image. Marketers engaged in branding seek to develop or align the expectations behind the brand experience, creating the impression that a brand associated with a product or service has certain qualities or characteristics that make it special or unique. This helps to answer the question of why a qualified candidate would seek employment there.

It is a law enforcement best practice to identify the particular niche of a law enforcement agency. The branding of your agency indicates the manner, style, or philosophy behind how your agency provides police services. It is the way in which you distinguish your agency from similar types of law enforcement agencies within your regional jurisdiction or state.

Some Marketing Tips

A customer (community member) orientation holds that success will come to that law enforcement organization that best determines the perceptions, needs, and wants of target markets (community stakeholders) and continually satisfies them through the design, communication, cost, and delivery of appropriate and competitively viable law enforcement service. Stated another way, the agency that succeeds is the one that best meets the needs and wants of its community members.

Advertising should be geared toward attracting the most qualified candidates. Ideally, you do not want "the best available" when you're recruiting you want "the best period." To do this, one needs to know what the most qualified candidates are seeking in a law enforcement career job. A law enforcement agency should develop an attractive, user friendly interactive job website for today's savvy qualified job seeker. This may require some research. In the process of developing a message, you will want to seek input from targeted groups to determine if the message will be received the way it is intended.

A Target Market Strategy

A law enforcement agency that wants to take a comprehensive and analytical approach to marketing could take this three-step approach:

- **Segmenting** — breaking down your total community service area into unique groups that respond like each other and differently from others.
- **Targeting** — choosing how to serve each of those segments (community service area) best given your resources (human, physical, and financial).
- **Positioning** — placing your department in a unique place in the mind of community members and policy makers.

Every law enforcement agency has both internal and external customers. The internal customers are other departments and elected officials within your jurisdiction. The external customers are community members and criminal justice agencies with whom the organization interfaces. Understanding your customers and their wants and needs, and maximizing your capacity for effective service delivery is foundational to your marketing strategy.

Another consideration is the medium used to advertise. A multi-faceted approach usually works best. Therefore, a combination of both print and electronic media should be used to advertise the law enforcement job. In a government job, the community should have both knowledge of and access to job openings. Advertise in ways that will reach the best candidates. Be mindful that historically most candidates hired live within a geographical radius of the agency. Determine the radius by surveying your current employees. Recruitment resources spent outside this radius are generally wasted. Develop a way to track which approach yields the best candidates. Employees are the best recruiters only if they know what qualities are desired.

All managers should be involved in the recruitment of law enforcement candidates. My bias is that managers should spend at least ten percent of their time searching for top law enforcement talent. One of the most significant contributions managers can make is to recruit an effective employee for their agency. Provide employees with materials that can be distributed to potential qualified candidates. Consider ways to acknowledge and/or reward employees who refer candidates who are hired by the agency. By developing and implementing such a policy you are both motivating employees while communicating to them what makes an effective officer.

Website Advertising of the Law Enforcement Job

Redesign the police department Internet website to make it more applicant friendly. Provide information about the law enforcement officer job and the application process.

It is recommended that the website be redesigned to add additional information in the following areas:

- **Application process.** The application process is currently included; however, it should be updated periodically and provide a timeline on the application periods identified to be selected for each class within a given calendar year. In other words, candidates should be able to figure out when they could potentially be hired.

- **Provide your background removal standards.** A brief overview of some critical background removal standards should be placed on the website to discourage unsuitable candidates from applying. Ideally, you want a pool of applicants without any preliminary disqualifiers. Review the information in the appendix for this chapter titled, "So you want to be a law enforcement officer?"

- **Out-of-state applicants.** Redesign the application process in such a way that out-of-state applicants can complete the process in no more than two visits. Information about this process should be placed on the website that clearly indicates what selection steps will be completed during each visit.

- **Create an online downloadable application.** If a full application is not utilized then create a pre-application to pre-screen candidates. It is recommended that, as part of the online process, candidates fill out a very short marketing survey that is included at the conclusion of the application to be completed. Some key information can be captured on a separate marketing document such as current job, place of residence, education, and why they selected to apply to this agency.

- **Provide candidates with information about the law enforcement profession.** The website "Discover Policing," which is funded by the Bureau of Justice Assistance and managed by the International Association of Chiefs of Police, is a recommended no-cost website to use by your agency to provide candidates with realistic and up-to-date information about the profession and your agency.

- **Include information about the agency's vision, mission, core values, and goal statements on the website.** Additionally, a statement from the law enforcement CEO, agency crime statistics, an organizational chart, and the community demographics will help prospective candidates evaluate if they are a good fit for your agency.

The Discover Policing Project

The Discover Policing project is a federally funded project by the Bureau of Justice Assistance and managed by the International Association of Chiefs of Police. It is a nationwide law enforcement recruitment initiative using a career information website as its cornerstone.

The project has three major goals:

First   Foster recruiting success for individual agencies and the profession of law enforcement.

Second   Provide job seekers with clear and accurate information on law enforcement career opportunities.

Third   Reach out and attract broad and diverse applicants, particularly those who may not otherwise consider a law enforcement career (COPS, Law Enforcement Recruitment Toolkit, 2009).

The career database is divided into four categories:

- Why policing?
- What's it like?
- What does it take?
- Finding your career.

One of the motivations for creating this website is to counter the image and perception of policing being crafted by the major media. It is time for the profession of law enforcement to create and manage its own image. The perception of the image of law enforcement affects the ability of law enforcement agencies to recruit qualified candidates of diverse populations.

The following is a summary of the key features of this website:

- Comprehensive, accurate information on law enforcement careers from a reliable, credible source.
- Searchable law enforcement job listings in all 50 states.

- The ability of job seekers to receive job alerts for notification of new listing.
- An anonymous resume bank helps connect potential candidates with hiring agencies.
- Profiles and testimonies from real officers.
- A nationwide directory of agency contact information.
- State by state information on officer requirements and standards.
- A recruiting events calendar for law enforcement agencies and candidates.

The purpose and features of Discover Policing are certainly helpful to achieve the recruitment goals of any law enforcement agency. It is recommended that all law enforcement agencies use this resource to assist in their advertisement of the law enforcement job.

Appendix 3-1
Are You Ready to Become
a Law Enforcement Officer?

Are you ready to work in an environment that fosters leadership, teamwork, and service to your community? Are you prepared to use innovative strategies to provide solutions to enhance citizen safety? Have you taken a moment to examine yourself to determine if you are the best law enforcement applicant you can be? Before you can become a law enforcement officer you will be required to undergo a background investigation. The purpose of a background investigation is to determine your job suitability based on character.

Law enforcement applicants will be placed under exacting scrutiny to determine their suitability for the position of American Peace Officer (law enforcement officer). Many things are taken into consideration when selecting an applicant to become an officer. One of the more important considerations is drug use. The Criminal Justice field is firmly committed to a drug free society and workplace. Law Enforcement Agencies closely scrutinize any prior unlawful drug use by applicants.

To determine whether you may meet our law enforcement agency's drug polices, please answer the following questions:

- Have you purchased or used marijuana or any illegal drug within the last year?
- Do you have any pattern of illegal drug use including marijuana in the past three (3) years?
- Have you used any illegal drug other than marijuana after your twenty-first birthday?
- Have you sold any illegal drug for profit?
- Have you ever used an illegal drug (no matter how many times or how long ago) while in a law enforcement or prosecutorial position, or in a position that carries with it a high level of responsibility or public trust?

If you answered YES to any of these questions, you should NOT apply for this law enforcement officer job. They are immediate disqualifiers.

A second key consideration is the candidate's past involvement in criminal activity. To help to determine your eligibility to apply please answer these questions:

- Have you admitted to or been convicted of an offense, as an adult defined a felony by the federal state or local government where the offense occurred?
- Do you have pattern of theft from an employer during the course of your employment as an adult?
- Have you committed any theft offense with the last three years that exceeds $500.00?

If you answered YES to any of these questions, you should NOT apply for this law enforcement officer job. They are immediate disqualifiers.

Prior to submitting an application for employment, law enforcement applicants should request a copy of their credit report. This will allow applicants to determine their current credit condition and take any corrective actions, if necessary.

Under the Fair Credit Reporting Act you can request and obtain a free credit report. This can be obtained from **https://www.annual creditreport.com/cra/index.jsp** or you may contact the major credit reporting agencies at **www.Experian.com**, **www.TransUnion.com**, or **www.Equifax.com**.

Other issues that applicants may want to consider are past employment history, contacts with law enforcement agencies, and domestic relations. Law enforcement organizations are seeking men and women with integrity and a commitment to providing quality service to citizens and keeping neighborhoods safe.

Recommendations and Key Points for Advertising the Law Enforcement Job

- Branding for law enforcement is a method of identifying the style and manner your agency does policing. It is the way in which you distinguish your agency from similar types of law enforcement agencies within your regional jurisdiction or state.
- Advertising should be geared toward attracting the most qualified candidates. Ideally, you do not want "the best available" when you're recruiting you want "the best period."
- A law enforcement agency should develop an attractive, user friendly interactive job website for today's savvy qualified job seeker.
- Know that historically most candidates hired by a law enforcement agency live within a geographical radius of the agency. Determine the radius by surveying your current employees. Recruitment resources spent outside this radius are generally wasted.
- Employees are the best recruiters only if they know what qualities are desired.
- All managers should be involved in the recruitment of law enforcement candidates. One of the most significant contributions a manager can make is to recruit an effective employee for their agency.
- Redesign the police department Internet website to make it more applicant friendly. Provide information about the law enforcement officer job and the application process.
- Create an online downloadable application. If a full application is not utilized, then create a pre-application to pre-screen candidates.
- It is recommended that, as part of the online process, candidates fill out a very short marketing survey that is included at the conclusion of the application to be completed.
- Include critical agency profile information on the website to help prospective decide if they are a good fit your organization.
- It is recommended that all law enforcement agencies use "Discover Policing" to assist in their advertisement of the law enforcement job.

References

COPS/IACP Leadership Project. (2009). *Law enforcement recruitment toolkit.* Office of Community Oriented Policing Services. U.S. Department of Justice.

IACP – Discoverpolicing.org

Chapter 4

Developing Recruitment Strategies

Properly Screen and Select Recruiters

Every law enforcement agency should develop and implement a written policy regarding the qualifications and training required for a recruiter of law enforcement applicants. Individuals selected to be recruiters should be among the agency's best and brightest, remembering that personnel selection issues are the single most important management task. Therefore, individuals selected to recruit officers must have the knowledge, skills, abilities, behaviors, and traits to be effective in this role. This should be a person who makes a positive impression wearing the agency's uniform, enjoys the profession, and is committed to the achievement of the agency's mission. The agency should match the diversity of recruiters with those who the agency wants to recruit. Every law enforcement recruiter should first have a desire to recruit potential applicants for the agency. The officer's years of service, assignments, education, their job performance in their current role, and written and oral communication skills are key selection criteria. To select a recruiter there must be a formal selection process that should be a part of the agency's general orders manual. This policy should make clear the qualifications and process of becoming a recruiter.

It is important that those selected as recruiters receive job-related training. Some of the topical areas to train recruiters should include, but not be limited to, the agency's organizational statements (i.e.: the agency's Vision, Mission, Core Values, etc.), customer service, human resource laws and guidelines, officer job description, flexible profile of effective candidates, agency standards on recruitment and selection, job qualifications, pay and benefits, and how to guide prospective candidates through the selection process. The mandated training program for all recruiters selected should be completed prior to beginning the recruitment assignment. Ideally, being a recruiter should be a full-time assignment for an officer. If this is not possible due to the agency's size, then an officer should be detailed to this assignment during the period of the recruitment process. This ensures that recruitment officers give full-time attention to this process during the recruiting period.

Here are some of the qualifications or skills that a recruiter should possess or be trained in:

- College degree
- Oral communication skills
- Planning and organizing skills
- Understanding of the law enforcement officer selection process
- Strong service orientation
- Knowledge of the law enforcement agency's general orders manual
- Written communication skills
- Knowledge of Human Resource laws related to recruitment and selection
- Marketing and advertising ability
- High moral character
- Diversity of recruiters to match applicant pool or culturally competent
- Performance driven / results oriented
- Public Relations skills

Do Targeted Selection

The challenge with the recruitment process is trying to find suitable candidates among the pool of potential candidates, which appears to be diminishing in quality. Law enforcement agencies must identify increasingly larger candidate pools to effectively identify the number of officers needed to fill vacancies. This is analogous to panning for gold during the western expansion of the United States in the 1800s. Individuals would sift through tons of dirt with a pan to find a few gold nuggets. This process of panning for gold is similar to searching for a few effective law enforcement candidates in the large candidate pool. You are not looking for dirt, you are looking for gold. Therefore, this process is very inefficient, resulting in a waste of time, money, and effort. An agency must first identify a flexible profile of an effective officer. In other words, what are the knowledge, skills, abilities, behaviors, and traits that make one effective on the job? That becomes the organization's target. Once an agency has identified the target, then they must be proactive in identifying individuals who match what they are looking for. This is what executive recruiters do. When working for a client agency, executive recruiters first write a profile of an effective job candidate. This information is received from the client agency. They then work to identify a pool of candidates that match this profile. The client agency then screens all the candidates who have the ability to do the job and select the most suitable candidate based on the organizational fit. This is what law enforcement agencies should do. Targeted selection is hard work. You first must know what you are looking for and then you must ask the question, "Where can this type of individual be found?" One way to think of recruitment is to understand that there is an effective recruitment triangle. There are three primary components of an effective recruitment process. First, you must identify a flexible profile of a qualified candidate. Second, an agency must have a position(s) vacancy to fill. Third, there must be qualified candidates. If you have all three then you have an effective recruitment process. The Appendix at the end of this chapter provides a diagram of the effective recruitment triangle.

I was recruited into law enforcement using this process. A recruiter with the Ohio State Highway Patrol provided a profile to my Criminal Justice professor in college and he recommended me and one other student as a match for the recruiter's profile. Interestingly enough, both of us were successful in the screening process. The recruiter was 100 percent effective using this methodology. I wonder how successful this recruiter would have been if he had established a temporary booth at the college student union to recruit trooper applicants? You can't hit a target that you cannot see. Chapter 1 discusses criteria to consider for selecting law enforcement officers.

Grow Your Own Officers

Of all the recruitment strategies that are utilized to hire effective law enforcement officers, in my opinion, none is more successful than growing your own. The strategy of growing your own officers involves identifying individuals too young to be law enforcement officers that meet all the agency's qualifications, and to develop and mentor them until they become of age to begin their career as law enforcement officers. A cadet program is a grow-your-own model. The hiring of individuals in a cadet program after high school provides education, experience, and training for these students. According to the Bureau of Labor Statistics, job growth for patrol law enforcement officers is expected to increase by 11 percent by 2016. This indicates opportunities for candidates and competition for law enforcement agencies hiring. A great way to get ahead of the competition is to identify qualified candidates before they are eligible to apply for a law enforcement job. This early hiring also helps ensure that these individuals avoid activity that would disqualify them as a law enforcement applicant. It is recommended that cadets are screened using the same hiring process components that are required for full-time officers. The rules and regulations regarding conduct for all officers should apply to the cadets. They simply lack the age to become law enforcement officers. A mini-academy should be developed to provide an orientation to your agency and law enforcement service. Cadets should be given regular assignments and be required to work 20 – 80 hours per month. College education should be encouraged and ideally there should be tuition reimbursement available to assist cadets in pursuing their law enforcement related degree program. If education is encouraged, the minimum of a two-year degree should be required. Physical fitness training and testing should be mandatory to remain in the program. Police agencies that allow officers to be hired at ages less than 21 should keep an individual in a program for at least 18 months. Because current performance will be the best indicator of future performance an observation period of at least 18 months is preferable for evaluating the individual's suitability for law enforcement service.

Recruit Year-round

A best practice in law enforcement recruitment is to search all year for law enforcement candidates. This is the ideal perspective because the goal is not to get the best candidates available at the time when you are recruiting; it is simply to get the best! This concept is rare in most law enforcement agencies, because they are only allowed to hire when there are vacancies consistent with their authorized manpower allocation. The agencies that are able to recruit year round are able to land quality law enforcement candidates when they find them. Remember the quality of your organization is reduced to the quality of your people. Organization growth and development is constrained by your ability to hire top talent. An agency needs to gain the ability to hire between five to ten percent over their established authorized strength depending on agency size. If hires can be made year-round, then an agency can hire quality candidates when they are identified. In most hiring processes, the time of the application to complete field training is typically 9 – 12 months. This means that waiting until vacancies occur create a long lag time before officers are available for patrol duty. Once candidates have been fully screened and hired, they should begin a formal orientation program and a job assignment while waiting for the next available basic recruit academy class.

Out-of-State Candidates

If an agency believes it is beneficial to recruit candidates, or has local candidates such as college students that temporarily reside out-of-state, then a process structure for these individuals is necessary. Sometimes qualified candidates are just interested in an out-of-state agency for a variety of reasons. In reality all law enforcement agencies have local candidates majoring in studies at colleges out-of-state that desire to become law enforcement officers. The idea is not to eliminate these candidates because the process is inaccessible to them during the hiring process. The strategy to overcome this challenge for out-of-state candidates is to allow candidates to complete the entire process within two visits. Two round-trip visits can be very expensive for a college student who is already overextended on college cost. My students have confirmed for me that more than two visits are very difficult to handle, especially if there is a great distance to travel to the agency. Therefore the selection process must be structured so that each component of the process (the same as the process for in-state candidates) so that they can be completed over multiple days during each visit. Identifying and summarizing this process on the agency website and other marketing material will be important to inform potential candidates temporarily or permanently residing out of state.

Duration of the Hiring Process

It is recommended that the entire hiring process for law enforcement officers never exceed four months or 16 weeks. Three months or 12 weeks is the ideal period of time. The process should be developed and structured so that it is clear at the beginning of the process when the hiring process begins and when it concludes. The specific dates for each component of the entire selection process should also be provided. This means the employer should clearly indicate to the candidates the requirements of the job, and the process for filling the job, including the timetable, in advance of the selection process. When applying for a job, one's life is somewhat on hold because most short-term and some long-term decisions are difficult to make, based on whether the applicant may or may not get the job. For many candidates, especially those most qualified, they are going to take the first job offered from these agencies where they have applied. Because applicants know they are not guaranteed to be hired, they will apply to multiple agencies where they have an interest. If the length of the process is unknown (which appears to be more common than uncommon), or unspecified, then candidates are both frustrated and left to wonder how to make key short-term and long-term decisions they are confronted with. The outcome of this situation is that the best candidates are either discouraged and leave the process, or they are hired by other agencies with hiring processes that are better prepared and planned. It is important to remember that while you are evaluating the candidates, they are also evaluating your agency. If people are the most important resource, and selecting them is the most important managerial task, then what do you communicate to prospective employees if the process is not clearly defined, not well organized, and lacking in candidate-specific information? It may seem like a difficult task to structure a complete hiring process within a three- to four-month period, but agencies that do so have a process structured to hire the most qualified candidates.

Hire Between June and September

There is a distinct advantage in catering your hiring process around the availability of college graduates. Those individuals with two-year or four-year academic degrees should be prepared with knowledge, skills, and abilities to enhance their law enforcement performance. Structuring the timing of your hiring process around the months immediately after college graduation will allow you to recruit the most qualified college applicants prior to your competition. Hiring candidates at the beginning of the calendar year might be an alignment with the fiscal budget period that starts at the same time, but not effective for attracting top college graduates. This post-graduation time period is important for college applicants and not essential for all other applicants. The official hiring date for the job applicants (which, in many cases, may be when the academy starts) should be between June and September. If an agency does not operate its own academy, candidates should begin their employment during this period awaiting the beginning of the basic recruit academy.

Provide Ride-alongs

Every applicant for a law enforcement job should have the opportunity to ride-along with experienced officers to gain a better understanding of the job. Unfortunately, some applicants lack a realistic understanding of what a law enforcement job entails. Many police administrators (myself included) have had the experience of recruiting and selecting a law enforcement officer who then completes the basic academy and field training, only to discover during their probationary period that they are not interested in the job. Candidates should be offered a ride-along opportunity to gain an understanding of both the job environment and requirements. An interview with feedback should be obtained from the candidate to evaluate their assessment of the ride-along experience and job environment. The purpose of the ride-along is to determine job compatibility.

Use College Interns

It is interesting to discover that many law enforcement agencies do not use college interns. Many colleges and universities with academic programs in law enforcement-related fields of study require that students have an internship in their major prior to graduation. Internships for college graduates have three benefits. One, students gain some job-related experience in their field of study. Two, students perform better in their courses because they can relate what they are learning to work as a practitioner. Three, students have a more realistic understanding of their career field. The law enforcement agencies using interns will be able to evaluate potential candidates separate from their involvement in the hiring process. The interns the agency becomes the most interested in can then be recruited for a law enforcement position. A law enforcement administrator should visit a local college or university and request to establish an interns program for students in law enforcement-related majors. In fact, the agency can request that the best students in this program apply for internship positions at their agency. Professors teaching in these academic programs will know which students are the highest performing academically, and most prepared for entry-level employment. Instead of waiting for college applicants to apply for law enforcement positions, local agency administrators can literally pick the fruit right off the tree. An internship program should be structured so that the intern has a job assignment within the agency while being provided overall exposure to the organization. By being structured in this way, it is a win-win arrangement for the student intern and the agency. Every law enforcement agency should take advantage of this opportunity to mine their local college or university for top talent.

Personalize the Recruitment Process

Every applicant in a law enforcement selection process should be assigned an officer to help facilitate the candidate's completion of the hiring process. This assigned recruiter becomes a point-of-contact for an applicant. Applicants have both questions and concerns when trying to navigate a law enforcement selection process. It is frustrating for candidates to not know who to call or what to do when trying to complete the application process. A primary and secondary point of contact for each applicant during the selection process helps to personalize this highly structured screening system. Recruiters should be provided a list of commonly asked questions by law enforcement applicants with answers. This information, along with effective screening requirements for police recruiters, will enable a recruiter to respond in an effective and efficient manner to applicant questions.

Every Manager is a Recruiter

Every individual law enforcement manager in an agency should also be a recruiter. Between five to ten percent of the law enforcement manager's time should be dedicated to the important task of finding top talent. Recruiting the most qualified police candidates is simply hard work. Simply marketing or advertising police vacancies is not recruitment. Effective recruitment, as previously stated, begins with knowing what type of person you are looking for and then being proactive to recruit that type of candidate in an environment in which he or she may be found. Identifying organizations and individuals that have knowledge of people who possess the qualities you are looking for is key. The professional law enforcement often issues "BOLOs" which means "be on the lookout for someone," they should always be on the lookout for top talent. This search for top law enforcement talent should be part of a manager's job description and included in their evaluation. The people hired are more important than any job function or task because it is the people who are hired that provide service to the community. Therefore, ideally, all managers should be recruiters.

Sell Community Service and Honor

The profession of law enforcement is both honorable and service-oriented. Whether it is a major city law enforcement agency, or a small rural law enforcement agency, service is what you sell. Law enforcement officers are mostly trained for enforcement, but provide mostly service. Most of the daily operational assignments and duties focus on service to the community. As mentioned in Chapter 1, service is one of the five most important traits of effective law enforcement officers. Those seeking a career of excitement (the action junkies) are individuals less suited for law enforcement. Because service-oriented law enforcement officers perform more effectively, it is those individuals who should be proactively recruited. From time-to-time, the badge of law enforcement has been tarnished by illegal or unethical behavior from officers on or off the job. Media reports of these incidents potentially create a perception of a dishonorable profession. Of course, law enforcement is, in fact, an honorable profession. Law enforcement agencies need to market to the small percentage of individuals qualified to perform this most important public service. Additionally, the power and authority granted law enforcement officers require that we recruit and hire men and women who are willing to serve with honor. The marketing of police officer vacancies should emphasize that it is an honorable job requiring a strong service orientation.

Factors that Hinder Law Enforcement Recruitment

The Office of Community Oriented Policing Services awarded a grant to the International Association of Chiefs of Police to study law enforcement recruitment. This resulted in a document titled, "Law Enforcement Recruitment Toolkit." In this document it summarized five key factors that hinder police recruitment. These five areas are factors that could discourage individuals who might otherwise apply for law enforcement work:

1. **Unfavorable Demographic and Social Trends** — Law enforcement executives report that many traditional applicants fail to qualify because of drug use and ethical concerns discovered during background investigations, psychological assessments, or polygraph exams.

2. **Lack of Diversity in Some Police Departments** — The underrepresentation of minorities and women police officers in some departments creates a shortage of role models for recruitment of these populations.

3. **Unattractiveness of Paramilitary Organizations** — The military appearance and structure of many police organizations is not always attractive to potential recruits who otherwise seek socially responsible work.

4. **Intense Competition for Candidates** — Law enforcement agencies are competing with private security firms and military recruiters for law enforcement candidates from the same labor pool.

5. **Bureaucratic and Burdensome Personnel Regulations** — Cumbersome civil service laws and difficult human resource practices make it challenging to design and implement a hiring process that selects high quality candidates.

These are issues that must be overcome through purposefully designing and implementing a hiring process that is both applicant friendly and accurately evaluates job-related skills and abilities.

Appendix 4-1
The Effective Recruitment Triangle

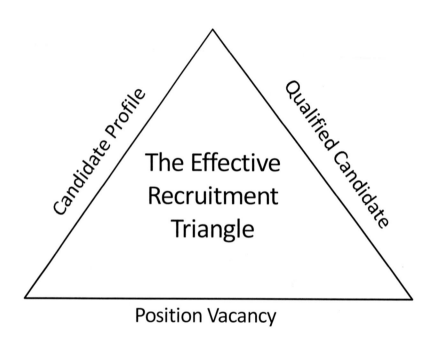

The Effective
Recruitment
Triangle

Candidate Profile

Qualified Candidate

Position Vacancy

Recommendations and Key Points of Developing Recruitment Strategies

- Every law enforcement agency should develop and implement a written policy regarding the qualifications and training required for a recruiter of law enforcement applicants.
- It is important that those selected as recruiters receive job-related training.
- Targeted selection is hard work. You first must know what you are looking for and then you must ask the question, "Where can this type of individual be found?"
- Of all the recruitment strategies that are utilized to hire effective law enforcement officers none is more successful than growing your own. The strategy of growing your own officers involves identifying individuals too young to be law enforcement officers that meet all the agency's qualifications, and to develop and mentor them until they become of age to begin their career as law enforcement officers.
- A best practice in law enforcement recruitment is to search all year for law enforcement candidates. The agencies that are able to recruit year round are able to land quality law enforcement candidates when they find them.
- Out-of-state law enforcement candidates should be allowed to complete the entire process within two visits.
- It is recommended that the entire hiring process of law enforcement officers never exceed four months or 16 weeks. Three months or 12 weeks is the ideal period of time.
- The employer should clearly indicate to the candidates the requirements of the job, and the process for filling the job, including the timetable, in advance of beginning the selection process.
- Structuring the timing of your hiring process the months immediately after college graduation will allow you to recruit the most qualified applicants prior to your competition.
- Every applicant for a law enforcement job should have the opportunity to ride along with experienced officers to gain a better understanding of the job to help determine compatibility.

- Every law enforcement agency should develop an internship program. It should be structured so that the intern has a job assignment within the agency while being provided overall exposure to the organization.
- Every applicant in a law enforcement selection process should be assigned an officer to help facilitate the candidate's completion of the hiring process.
- Every individual law enforcement manager in an agency should also be a recruiter. Between five to ten percent of the law enforcement manager's time should be dedicated to the important task of finding top talent.
- Every individual law enforcement manager in an agency should also be a recruiter. Between five to ten percent of the law enforcement manager's time should be dedicated to the important task of finding top talent.
- The marketing of police officer vacancies should emphasis that is an honorable job requiring a strong service orientation.
- Law enforcement agencies should work to avoid the five key factors that hinder law enforcement recruitment.

References

COPS/IACP Leadership Project. (2009). *Law enforcement recruitment toolkit.* Office of Community Oriented Policing Services. U.S. Department of Justice.

Chapter 5

Building Community
Partnerships for Recruitment

Why Community Partnerships

Effective recruitment requires that law enforcement agencies build strong partnerships with multiple segments of the community. In an era of community-based policing it should be well understood that law enforcement agencies are more effective when they work in partnership with the community they serve. The members of a community have a stake in the quality of officers hired to serve in their community. If law enforcement agencies reach out to various segments of the community for assistance in the recruitment and selection of law enforcement officers they will likely receive a positive response.

Benefits of Engaging the Community

According to the Office of Community Oriented Policing Services Office, engaging the community in the recruitment and selection process has at least six general benefits:

1. More can be accomplished together that either group could accomplish alone.
2. Working together will prevent duplication of individual or group efforts.
3. Collaboration will enhance the power of advocacy and resource development.
4. Joint efforts create more public visibility for the recruitment process.
5. Community involvement will provide a more systematic and comprehensive approach to the recruitment and selection challenges.
6. Working together on the initiative could create more opportunities for collaboration on future projects

The next logical question is who are the key members of the community that a law enforcement agency should seek to partner with on recruitment and selection? Each agency should develop their own comprehensive list of community contacts that can help facilitate an effective recruitment and selection process. The following is a list of recommended community leaders or organizations that a law enforcement agency might partner with:

- The community's elected officials
- Business owners and associations
- The faith/community
- The local school district
- Military leaders
- College and University faculty and staff
- Minority advocacy groups
- Non-profit organizations
- Social Service organizations
- Philanthropic organizations
- Community leaders
- Criminal justice organizations

The goal is to develop relationships with these community groups or individuals that will provide a potential pipeline of the most qualified candidates. Because it has been previously recommended that every manager should be a recruiter the idea is to build formal relationships between leaders in each organization and members of your management and recruitment team. Individuals and organizational leaders need to understand both the profile of an effective law enforcement officer and the purpose and structure of the selection process.

A Recruitment and Retention Advisory

A law enforcement agency should establish a recruitment and retention advisory council whose members represent a cross section of businesses, private and public organizations, community leaders, and other stakeholders receiving law enforcement services. This advisory council is committed and dedicated to an active partnership with the law enforcement agency. The purpose of the council is to facilitate the recruitment and retention of high-quality applicants.

Ideally, prior to serving on the advisory council, these individuals should attend an agency-sponsored citizen's police academy to become familiar with the organization's missions and goals. An academy may or may not be required; however, it is a great method to prepare advisory council members for involvement with the law enforcement agency. If an agency currently has a citizen's academy, it is a useful tool to screen, train, and prepare volunteers for service on the advisory council. A minimum of quarterly meetings for the advisory council is necessary to maintain momentum and achieve the agency's recruitment goals.

Additional Considerations

A law enforcement agency must particularly focus on building formal partnerships within segments of the community that either contains potential law enforcement candidates or that can help identify potential law enforcement candidates. These community partners must understand the flexible profile of a law enforcement officer. The representatives of the law enforcement agency must be intentional and focus their recruitment efforts with people and agencies likely to yield the best results. Developing rapport with these liaison agencies also facilitates referring candidates that are not a good match for your agency to a more compatible organization for possible employment.

The law enforcement agency should recruit from private and public sales and service organizations. Qualified individuals from private and public sales and service organizations can possess several qualities that make someone an effective law enforcement officer. The skill set, interest, personality, and values of an effective law enforcement candidate are the traits that make one effective in other career fields and occupations. Therefore, the following characteristics (as previously indicated), which make someone effective as a law enforcement officer, are also found among effective sales and service employees:

- **Integrity** — The candidate has a high moral character in all matters private and public.
- **Service orientation** — The candidate has a desire and commitment of service to others above self.

- **Interpersonal relations** — The candidate has the ability to interact effectively with people.
- **Team compatibility** — The candidate has the ability to work with others in a supportive manner to achieve the goals of the group.
- **Performance-driven** — The candidate has the desire and motivation to be successful in achieving individual and group goals.

Candidates from private and public sales and service organizations who possess these qualities should be actively recruited for law enforcement positions. It is a law enforcement best practice to actively solicit the applications of qualified candidates who might not otherwise apply. This strategy can be highly effective if the sales or service organization knows what the law enforcement agency is looking for. There are five key qualities that should be used to evaluate candidates from sales and service organizations to determine their potential effectiveness as a law enforcement officer. Managers of these employees should be asked about these qualities in relation to their job performance.

Recommendations and Key Points of Building Community Partnerships

1. Effective recruitment requires that law enforcement agencies build strong partnerships with multiple segments of the community.
2. If law enforcement agencies reach out to various segments of the community for assistance in the recruitment and selection of law enforcement officers, they will likely receive a positive response.
3. According to the Office of community Oriented Policing Services Office, engaging the community in the recruitment and selection process has at least six general benefits.
4. Each agency should develop their own comprehensive list of community contacts that can help facilitate an effective recruitment and selection process.
5. The goal is to develop relationships with these community groups or individuals that will provide a potential pipeline of the most qualified candidates.

6. A law enforcement agency should establish a recruitment and retention advisory Council whose members represent a cross section of businesses, private and public organizations, community leaders, and other stakeholders receiving law enforcement services. This is an advisory council that is committed and dedicated to an active partnership with the law enforcement agency, facilitating the recruitment and retention of high-quality applicants.

7. Ideally prior to serving on the advisory council, these individuals should attend an agency-sponsored citizen's police academy to become familiar with the organization's missions and goals.

8. Developing rapport with these liaison agencies also facilitates referring candidates that are not a good match for your agency to a more compatible organization, for possible employment.

9. There are five key qualities which should be used to evaluate candidates from sales and service organizations to determine their potential effectiveness as a law enforcement officer. Managers of these employees should be asked about these qualities in relation to their job performance.

References

COPS/IACP Leadership Project (2009). *Law enforcement recruitment toolkit*. Office of Community Oriented Policing Services. U.S. Department of Justice.

Chapter 6

Analyzing the Recruitment Process

What Works in Recruitment

Every law enforcement agency should determine how effective they currently are in the recruitment of quality applicants. Before effective changes can be made in the recruitment process the agency's current efforts must be analyzed. How much does your agency know about the success of past recruitment efforts and the viability of current methods, processes, or strategies? How much effort is there to better understand the agency, community, and candidate pool? Your research for example should provide an agency with information to aid in answering the following questions: What are the qualities of the ideal candidate? Are the current job qualifications compatible with the agency's needs? What advertising and other efforts are yielding the best results? What are the agency's officer demographics, and how do they compare with the community served? What has attracted and kept existing staff? What were the geographical locations of current officers prior to being hired? Why do officers leave the agency? Are your pay and benefits compatible with similar agencies within the geographic area? How long does it take candidates to complete the selection process once begun? What do candidates like and dislike about the recruitment and selection process? What policies and procedures should be changed to make the process more effective? The answers to these and other relevant questions will impact the development of an agency's recruitment, selection, and retention strategic plan.

The Effective Use of Data

As a consumer of goods and services all of us have loyalty cards from places where we shop. These loyalty cards provide discounts for purchasing certain products or services. They have two primary functions: *first*, to keep us as repeat customers and *second*, to record our shopping habits at that establishment. It is the latter function of these cards that is the most beneficial to the organization. This data provides valuable information that can be used to make more effective organizational decisions. It helps businesses to know what is purchased, in what quantities, how often, during what times, and so on. This information is collected by organization and then effectively analyzed for decision-making. The collection and analyzing of data has become an essential element for high-performing organizations. Law enforcement agencies today commonly perform the crime analysis function or use intelligence-led policing strategies. Agencies using these strategies operate under the principle that the effective collection and analyzing of data improves the quality of decision making. Regardless of an individual or groups, organizational knowledge, skill, or ability data analysis provides information that would otherwise be unknown. Effective data analysis can prove or disprove organizational theories or assumptions. Simply restated, the most effective managers use data to improve the quality of their decision making. Critical organizational decisions should be supported and enhanced by sound research. Law enforcement agencies should analyze their recruitment efforts to determine both the success of past recruitment efforts and identify more effective policies, strategies, and methods.

It is a law enforcement best practice to determine the geographic radius in which you are most likely to select law enforcement candidates. It is important to understand the geographical radius in which an agency most effectively can market and advertise vacant positions for law enforcement officers. The collection of research data from your current officers will provide a historical perspective on the quality of your candidate pool.

An agency should develop and conduct a survey of all officers hired for the last three years to continue to analyze this information. In the Appendix at the end of this chapter is a basic model of a recruitment survey that an agency may use to collect recruitment data. Continue to conduct ongoing studies on your law enforcement recruits to use this data for more effective decision making.

Appendix 6-1
Recruit Survey

1. What is your gender?   ☐ MALE   ☐ FEMALE

2. What is your current age? ☐ 18 - 29 ☐ 30 - 39 ☐ 40 - 49 ☐ 50 +

3. Which of the following best describes your highest level of education? [check ONE only]

    ☐   High School Graduate or GED
    ☐   Some college, but less than 60 units
    ☐   AA or completion of 60 units of college
    ☐   BA degree
    ☐   Post-Graduate degree

4. What job were you doing professionally prior to being hired?
    _____

5. Where did you live before being hired?
    _____   _____   _____
    CITY   COUNTY   STATE

6. Did you relocate [move] to accept this position? ☐ YES ☐ NO

To what extent do you disagree or agree with the statements listed in #7 & #8, using this scale:

STRONGLY DISAGREE	DISAGREE	SOMEWHAT DISAGREE	NO OPINION	SOMEWHAT AGREE	AGREE	STRONGLY AGREE
1	2	3	4	5	6	7

7. I pursued a job in ___ law enforcement agency for the following reasons: [CIRCLE your response]

a. Stable employment	1	2	3	4	5	6	7
b. Salary & Benefits	1	2	3	4	5	6	7
c. Retirement Plan	1	2	3	4	5	6	7
d. Adventure/Excitement	1	2	3	4	5	6	7
e. Desire to serve	1	2	3	4	5	6	7
f. Shift work	1	2	3	4	5	6	7
g. Non-routine work	1	2	3	4	5	6	7
h. Independence	1	2	3	4	5	6	7
i. Status of being a police officer	1	2	3	4	5	6	7
j. Other [Please specify in the box below.]	1	2	3	4	5	6	7

8. The following aspects of applying for a police officer position with ___ agency were difficult for me.

a. Finding out when the test would be given	1	2	3	4	5	6	7
b. Completing the application	1	2	3	4	5	6	7
c. Meeting minimum requirements for the position	1	2	3	4	5	6	7
d. Written test	1	2	3	4	5	6	7
e. Oral interview	1	2	3	4	5	6	7
f. Physical agility	1	2	3	4	5	6	7
g. Background investigation	1	2	3	4	5	6	7
h. Medical exam	1	2	3	4	5	6	7
i. Psychological screening	1	2	3	4	5	6	7
j. Time involved to complete the process	1	2	3	4	5	6	7
k. Lack of contact through the process	1	2	3	4	5	6	7
l. Other [Please specify in the box below.]	1	2	3	4	5	6	7

9. I was recruited to this agency via: [check ALL that apply]

☐   a. Self-referral
☐   b. Job fair
☐   c. Agency employee who is a friend or relative
☐   d. Agency employee who told me about the opportunity
☐   e. Ad in newspaper
☐   f. Ad on radio/television
☐   g. Website
☐   h. Friend/family not in law enforcement referred me
☐   i. Friend/family who works in a different law enforcement agency
☐   j. I was already with the agency in another capacity
☐   k. Other [Please specify in the box below.]

To what extent do you agree or disagree with the statements listed in #10, using this scale:

STRONGLY DISAGREE	DISAGREE	SOMEWHAT DISAGREE	NO OPINION	SOMEWHAT AGREE	AGREE	STRONGLY AGREE
1	2	3	4	5	6	7

10. I accepted employment with this agency because:

a.	Size of agency	1	2	3	4	5	6	7
b.	First agency to offer me a position	1	2	3	4	5	6	7
c.	Location of city or agency	1	2	3	4	5	6	7
d.	Affordability of housing	1	2	3	4	5	6	7
e.	Salary/Benefits	1	2	3	4	5	6	7
f.	Reputation of the agency	1	2	3	4	5	6	7
g.	Friend/family works for this agency	1	2	3	4	5	6	7
h.	Retirement plan	1	2	3	4	5	6	7
i.	Variety in assignments	1	2	3	4	5	6	7
j.	Work hours available to me, such as 10 or 12 hour shifts	1	2	3	4	5	6	7
k.	I was already with the agency in another capacity	1	2	3	4	5	6	7
l.	Other [Please specify in the box below.]	1	2	3	4	5	6	7

11. How would you rate the starting pay rate compared to other large state or local law enforcement agencies in the region?

    ☐ HIGH   ☐ MEDIUM   ☐ LOW

12. Give the THREE best attributes of the agency:

    1. _____
    2. _____
    3. _____

13. Identify three areas that need improvement in the agency.

    _____
    _____
    _____

14. What three areas or issues might be improved regarding the law enforcement officer recruitment and selection process?

    _____
    _____
    _____

Recommendations and Key Points of Analyzing the Recruitment Process

1. Every law enforcement agency should determine how effective they currently are in the recruitment of quality applicants. Before effective changes can be made in the recruitment process the agency's current efforts must be analyzed.
2. Key questions need to be answered regarding the ideal qualifications of an effective law enforcement officer that are compatible with the agency needs.
3. The agency should understand what has attracted and kept existing staff.
4. The agency should understand how long it takes candidates to complete the selection process.
5. The agency should determine what candidates like and dislike about the current selection process.
6. The agency should collect data to analyze for decisions concerning the hiring process.
7. It is a law enforcement best practice to determine the geographic radius in which you are most likely to select law enforcement candidates.
8. An agency should develop and conduct a survey of all officers hired for the last three years to continue to analyze this information.

Chapter 7

The Role of College Education

The topic of the value of college education in relation to job performance has been discussed, debated, and researched for over 100 years in the profession of law enforcement (yes, 100 years). Unfortunately, this topic is still debated at the state and local level of law enforcement. To effectively recruit and retain law enforcement officers one of the key issues all agencies must determine is, what is the organization's position on the college education for its officers? This is a topic that must be addressed to understand its role on the recruitment, selection, and retention of law enforcement officers.

A Police Executive Research Forum (PERF) (Carter, Sapp, & Stephens, 1986) hypothesized several advantages of college education for police officers:

- It provides a broader base of knowledge for decision-making.
- The academic program requirements provide the individual with a greater appreciation for and understanding of constitutional rights, values, and the democratic form of government.
- College education makes individuals more creative and innovative.
- Those with a higher education tend to be more effective with diverse populations.
- The college-educated officer is assumed to be more flexible in decision-making and adapts more readily to organizational change.
- The college experience helps officers to communicate more effectively.

What Does Some of the Research Evidence Indicate?

In a 2002 Florida study ("Does Higher Education mean a Lower Risk of Disciplinary Action?" 2002), it indicated that police officers with just a high school diploma made up more than half of all law enforcement personnel in the state, yet they accounted for almost 75 percent of all the disciplinary actions. This study, which was commissioned by the International Association of Chiefs of Police, also found that the severity of discipline imposed was related to their educational levels.

An article published by the Journal of Criminal Justice Education (Polk, 2001) indicated that higher education reduces the time required for promotion and assignment to specialized positions for law enforcement officers. The implication of this study is that higher education will enhance an officer's probability of rising in rank regardless of whether the agency requires a college degree as a pre-condition of employment.

A study published by Public Personnel Management (Truxillo, Bennett, & Collins, 1998) presents evidence of a positive relationship between college education and police job performance. In an organization where college education was not formally supported by the promotional system, this study investigated the relationship between measures of college education and work performance for a cohort of 84 officers over a ten-year period. College-educated officers were promoted more often and had higher supervisory ratings of job knowledge.

The findings of *Policing: An International Journal of Police Strategies & Management* (Carlan, 2006) indicates that officers with Criminal Justice degrees perceive their education substantially improved their knowledge and abilities in a wide range of areas from the criminal justice system to conceptual and managerial skills. This study was done in the state of Alabama involving 16 law enforcement agencies with 50 or more sworn officers in which 1,114 officers participated.

The findings of an article entitled "Higher Education and Policing: Where are We Now?" (Roberg & Bonn, 2004) concludes that it appears there is enough evidence (both empirical and experimental) has been established to support the argument for a college-degree requirement for entry-level law enforcement officers. It additionally indicates that, if education and recruitment policies are appropriately developed and implemented, higher education requirement should not have an adverse affect upon minority recruitment or retention.

A Chief's Perspective on Higher Education

Over the past 20 years, I've had the opportunity to discuss the issue of higher education and its relationship to job performance for law enforcement officers. During that time, I have developed a philosophy indicating why college education should be supported and encouraged in a law enforcement agency. I realize and understand that I am presenting my bias on this issue. However, the previous research provided, I think, supports the position I have taken.

First, as the Chief Executive Officer (CEO) of a law enforcement agency, there is only one of two messages you can send your staff on the issue of higher education. One message is that education is important and valued in the organization. The other message is that education is not important and not valued in the organization. One of these two messages will be communicated based on the agency's policies and practices regarding higher education. If a law enforcement CEO is trying to build a learning organization, I think there is only one legitimate choice and that is to support higher education. If there are not any requirements, benefits, or rewards for obtaining a college degree in your law enforcement agency, then officers that have or obtained a degree transition to a job where it has value. When the CEO takes a position of supporting higher education, those who disagree with this position, would say that this would have the potential of creating a negative environment for those without a college education. Keeping in mind that you must take one position or the other regarding higher education, here is the dilemma. You can risk offending those without a college education by supporting and encouraging it, or you can risk offending those with a college education by not supporting and encouraging it. Remember, you cannot be neutral on this issue. Your policies and practices will indicate whether you support and encourage college education or you do not. An officer who goes to college for six years part-time to finish a degree only to realize that the organization does not value his or her professional development can be discouraging. Please understand that I think it's important to value all of your officers whether they are college educated or not. However, from an organizational perspective, professional development should include college education.

Second, in past situations involving the hiring, assignment, or promotion of an officer, education tends to be a factor in one's performance in these competitive personnel selection decisions. Rarely, when making these personnel selection decisions, is it a choice between an incompetent and educated individual versus a competent and uneducated individual. My experience has been that all of the candidate finalists are competent and some stand out based on their education and training.

Third, the job of a law enforcement officer is becoming so complex from a technical, legal, social, and political perspective that officers with college educations are generally better prepared to be more effective on the job. Ideally, when hiring law enforcement officers, one wants to attract and select leadership talent. The majority of the future leadership of the law enforcement agency will come from officers hired at the entry level.

Finally, there are four positions a law enforcement agency can take on the issue of college education as an entry-level requirement. One, no college education is required for law enforcement officer candidates. Two, some college is required, such as a number of college credits equal to one year of education. Third, a degree, such as an associates, bachelors, or masters is required for law enforcement officer candidates. Four, the minimum of a baccalaureate degree is required.

My personal recommendation is that law enforcement agencies have a college degree requirement (associate or bachelors) for entry-level positions. It is interesting to note that nearly 25 percent of Americans today have at least a four-year level degree or higher. A legitimate question to ask is, "Is law enforcement keeping pace with societal trends in higher education?" Obviously, every law enforcement agency must decide what position it's going to take on this issue. Whatever position a law enforcement agency takes, ideally, it should be based on the organization's vision, mission, core values, major goals, and supported by research. It is therefore recommended that all law enforcement agencies create policies and guidelines on the role of education in their agency.

The Essential Outcomes of a College Education

As a university professor, I have been asked on several occasions about the benefits of a college education. Some prospective students and their parents have indicated they are aware that a college education is not required to apply to most state and local law enforcement agencies. Because that is true, they want to know why they should pursue a degree, and how it will benefit the student in their aspiration of a law enforcement career. This is a very good question that deserves a good answer. I have used the metaphor of being coached and trained for a marathon. All things being equal, a person who has been coached and trained for a marathon should do much better than one who has not. A marathon, which is a 26-mile race, is one based on the runner's preparedness and endurance. Likewise, a person must be prepared for a career that usually lasts 40 – 50 years minimum. The job of a college is to prepare the student for career success with the tools needed in an ever changing job market. These job-related knowledge, skills, and abilities need to be practical, flexible, and performance enhancing. Every college must ask the question: *How are we preparing our students and why?* To answer this question I use a document that addresses what I believe are the most essential outcomes of a college education. These can also be viewed as the benefits of a college education. These ten essential learning outcomes for college graduates are why law enforcement agencies should prefer college graduates. These benefits generally must apply to any profession or industry that a college student may pursue. The specific academic program should also teach and prepare students with knowledge, skills, and abilities related to that field of study.

10 Essential Learning Outcomes
For College Graduates

Graduates should be able to:

1. Communicate effectively, utilizing listening, speaking, reading, and writing skills.
2. Use quantitative analytical skills to evaluate and process numerical data.
3. Solve problems through critical thinking, creative thinking, and scientific reasoning.
4. Formulate strategies to locate, evaluate, and apply information.
5. Demonstrate knowledge of diverse cultures, including global and historical perspectives.
6. Create strategies that can be used to fulfill personal, civic, and social responsibilities.

7. Demonstrate knowledge of ethical thinking and its application to issues in society.
8. Use computer and emerging technologies effectively.
9. Demonstrate appreciation for aesthetics and creative activities.
10. Describe how natural systems function and recognize the impact of humans on the environment.

Recommendations and Key Points of the Role of Education in Recruiting and Retaining Law Enforcement Officers

1. Every law enforcement CEO has to make a decision on the role of education in their law enforcement agency. Either education is promoted and supported or it is not.
2. Based on several research studies conducted on the value of higher education there is evidence to support that higher education is advantageous to a law enforcement officer.
3. A ten-year study of officers indicated that college-educated officers were promoted more often and had higher supervisory ratings of job knowledge.
4. If education and recruitment policies are appropriately developed and implemented, higher education requirement should not have an adverse effect on minority recruitment or retention.
5. The job of a law enforcement officer is becoming so complex from a technical, legal, social, and political perspective that officers with college education are generally better prepared to be more effective on the job.
6. The majority of the future leadership of the law enforcement agency will come from officers hired at the entry level.
7. Nearly 25 percent of Americans today have at least a four-year level degree or higher.
8. It is recommended that all law enforcement agencies create policies and guidelines on the role of education in their agency.
9. The job of a college is to prepare the student for career success with the tools needed in an ever-changing job market. These job-related knowledge, skills, and abilities need to be practical, flexible, and performance enhancing.
10. There are ten key essential learning outcomes of a college education that make college graduates more desirable applicants.

References

Carlan, P. E. (2006). The criminal justice degree and policing: Conceptual development or occupational primer? *Policing: An International Journal of Police Strategies & Management,* 30, 608 – 619.

Carter, D. L. Sapp, A. D., & Stephens, D. W. (1986). The state of police education: police direction for the 21st century. Washington: Police Executive Research Forum.

"For Florida Police, Higher Education Means Lower Risk of Disciplinary Action," *Law Enforcement News,* October 2002, pp. 1 and 10.

Polk, O. E. & Armstrong, D. A. (2001). Higher education and law enforcement career paths: Is the road to success paved by degree? *Journal of Criminal Justice Education,* 12, 77 – 99.

Roberg, R. & Bonn, S. (2004). Higher education and policing: Where are we now? *Policing: An International Journal of Police Strategies & Management,* 27, 469 – 486.

Truxillo, D. M., Bennett, S. R., & Collins, M. L. (1998). College Education and Police Job Performance: A Ten-Year Study. *Public Personnel Management,* 27, 269 – 280.

Chapter 8

Why Have a
Multicultural Workforce?

The singular purpose of this chapter is to answer the question why a law enforcement agency should recruit and select a diverse workforce. Many law enforcement agencies are struggling with the issues of both why and how to diversify their workforce. Is it simple political correctness or does it enhance the performance of the agency? If an agency decides to diversify their workforce, how should they go about it and why? This chapter will answer these basic, but essential, questions for every law enforcement agency regarding diversity and hiring.

The word "diversity" has many interpretations. It can be interpreted broadly to describe any difference between people or so narrowly as to be limited to differences of gender and race. For the purpose of this book, diversity is defined as the variation of social and cultural identities among people existing together in a defined employment setting. In this definition, the phrase social and cultural identity refers to the personal affiliations with groups that research has shown to have significant influence on people's major life experiences. These affiliations include gender, race, national origin, religion, age cohort, and work specialization among others. As a characteristic of work groups, diversity creates challenges and opportunities that are not present in homogeneous work groups. To effectively manage diversity, an organization must understand its potential and performance barriers. Although the existence of diversity in the workplace is now widely recognized in organizations throughout the world, it is too often viewed only in terms of legal compliance in human rights protection. In reality, the implications of the diversity are much more demanding and much more interesting. Increasing diversity presents a double-edged sword. The challenge of managing diversity is to create conditions that minimize its potential to be a performance barrier while maximizing its potential to enhance organizational performance (Cox, Jr., 2001).

Cultural diversity is by no means a new phenomenon; it is a fact of life. The world has gradually come to America and daily life now includes the likelihood of encountering cultural diversity to a degree unparalleled in our history. Law enforcement, which is a public-sector profession spanning diverse communities, should lead the way in demonstrating to other professions how effective diverse organizations can and should be. I assert that an organization that is culturally diverse will be more functional, effective, and cohesive. Achieving cultural or ethnic diversity is the primary challenge for law enforcement with regards to recruitment, selection, and retention, not so much other aspects of diversity.

As early as the 1600s, people migrated to the United States with the hope for a better life, a better future for themselves and their families. They came here seeking religious liberty and freedom with the exceptions of those brought here as slaves. All those who immigrate here seek to be treated with dignity and respect. The United States of America is the most culturally diverse nation on Earth. On all of our U.S. currency, this phrase appears "E Pluribus Unum" which means "Out of many, one." This Latin phrase describes that, out of many cultures, we are one people or nation. It is the American belief that there is great strength in diversity. Do our law enforcement agencies that operate in a diverse community model this vision? Care must be taken to identify ways to involve all the ethnic groups of the community in our organization. We must learn to value ethnic diversity.

The most popular paragraph of our Declaration of Independence states, "We hold these Truths to be self-evident, that all Men are created equal, that they are endowed by their Creator with certain unalienable Rights that among these are Life, Liberty and the Pursuit of Happiness." These rights are unalienable because they were not given by man; therefore cannot be taken by man; they are God-given rights. Many Americans are familiar with this statement. Interestingly, many Americans (including law enforcement officers) are unaware of the words that immediately follow this statement. The Declaration goes on to say ... "That to secure these rights, governments were instituted among Men, deriving their just powers from the consent of the governed, That whenever any Form of Government becomes destructive to these ends, it is the Right of People to alter or to abolish it"... It does indicate that our government is instituted to secure these rights! If government fails to establish these rights then the people have the right to alter or abolish it. Therefore it is the responsibility of government to see that all are treated in accordance with the dictates of the Constitution. To maintain this vision of individual liberty, the protection of rights, individual pursuit of happiness requires the support of American law enforcement. The most fundamental purpose of law enforcement is to protect the constitutional rights of every individual. It is difficult for law enforcement to support these ideals if it does not believe in or model them. It is important to understand that our Constitution promotes equal opportunity for citizens.

To enhance the protection of constitutional rights, the workforce should reflect the ethnicity of the community. This is the catalyst for improving the relationship between the law enforcement agency and various segments of the community. Poor law enforcement/community relations hinder the recruitment of qualified applicants. It is difficult to develop strong positive community relations in the minority community without treating the cause—a lack of human diversity within the law enforcement agency. Each ethnic group has different backgrounds, perspectives, knowledge, skills, and experiences that are instrumental in improving the effectiveness of an organization. It would be prudent for law enforcement agencies to embrace diversity—a stepping stone to creating trust among the minority members of the community.

The chief's role is to provide strong leadership and to recognize the opportunities posed by increasing diversity. He or she must believe in and value a diverse organization. Developing and implementing cultural diversity in an organization is a philosophy that must be leader-led. If the law enforcement CEO and the leadership team do not support this initiative, it is doomed to fail. A tangible benchmark would be to achieve a composition of diversity in law enforcement agencies that is consistent with the ethnicity of the community. Additionally, employees must be held accountable for diversity in hiring, assignments, training, and promotion. It is highly recommended that a chief should mandate diversity training for all employees and provide updated in-service training on this topic each year. This training plan should describe and explain the agency's affirmative action plan and include the strategies to be used for its achievement. The training should also be inextricably linked to an understanding and application of the Constitution of the United States to law enforcement intervention with members of the community. The chief must ensure that the organizational policies, procedures, rules, and regulations reflect the organization's philosophy and practices concerning human diversity. Employees and managers alike must be held accountable for compliance with these mandates. This is not for the purpose of elevating one culture over another, but respecting and valuing all cultures and protecting their constitutional rights. This means rewarding those who support the philosophy and penalizing those who do not.

Strategies and a Strategic Plan for Creating a Multicultural Organization

What are the activities and actions necessary to create an effective multicultural organization? I believe an effective multicultural organizational change process should include at least five components. These components are:

- Leadership
- Planning and Research
- Training and Education
- Policy and Management Controls
- Follow-up and Feedback System

An overview will be provided for each one of the five processes to discuss its purpose, structure, and strategy implementation.

Leadership

Any major organizational change is a test of organizational leadership. One of the greatest organizational endeavors that can be undertaken today is to create an effective multicultural workplace. To achieve this change of the organizational culture requires the process be understood and led by the law enforcement Chief Executive Officer (CEO). The CEO must establish a clear vision for creating this multicultural organization. This vision will result in the identification of organizational goals. The CEO should articulate his or her organizational philosophy in regard to the purpose, value, and standards for creating a multicultural community. The CEO must demonstrate personal involvement and commitment to the success of this organizational change. This requires that the CEO also develop and implement a communications strategy that clearly articulates what is to be done and why. A separate strategic plan should be developed to effectively integrate multicultural staff hired into the agency.

Planning and Research

The CEO should begin with an audit of the agency to determine the current multicultural environment. Demographic information should also be collected about the service population to determine the ethnicity and cultural identities present. A plan should be developed to determine how incremental progress will measure against predetermined goals. It is recommended that the agency utilize the services of a professor from a local college or university to help conduct the organizational audit and conduct a community assessment. Often times, professors are willing to provide this service at no cost as part of a research for tenure or as part of their career development.

Training and Education

Is it possible that a major cultural change may occur in an organization without an intensive effort to help people learn new information and develop skills? A change conducted in this manner is highly unlikely to be successful. Training and education are a prerequisite to effectively manage a major change effort. Both education, which is "why to do" and training, which are "how to do," are essential components of an agency's multicultural implementation strategy. The focus of the training is on the purpose, philosophy, and goals of achieving a multi cultural workforce within your law enforcement agency. Education should provide some research and data that demonstrate the competitive edge of multicultural organizations. Training should be designed to provide some skills in areas such as recruiting, selecting, and managing in a multicultural workplace. Training and education must include every member of the organization with a primary emphasis on all managers.

Policies and Management Controls

A law enforcement agency striving to achieve a multicultural workplace must develop and implement an affirmative action plan. This plan provides a snapshot of the organization's multicultural diversity at a given point in time that provides a strategy to achieve predetermined goals. Of course, every organization should have an established policy on sexual and other forms of harassment that helps to establish accountability for all agency employees. In the law enforcement agency's General Orders Manual, it should contain an overview of the agency's philosophy and standards for a multicultural environment. A management controls system must be instituted in areas such as hiring, assignment, promotion, supervision, and performance appraisal to create an effective multicultural workplace. All managers should be evaluated in part on their progress toward established diversity goals. In other words, these management functions must be aligned with the goals of leveraging diversity.

Follow-up and Feedback System

This component involves developing and implementing a multicultural action plan. This plan assigns responsibility for specific tasks. However, all managers must have a role in creating a multicultural workplace. There should be a method for evaluating and establishing accountability for results. This component must overlap with the other four strategies but is especially linked with the affirmative action plan. This component must measure the degree to which predetermined goals are achieved and allow for corrective action.

Theoretical Perspective of Diversity and Affirmative Action

Affirmative action policies originated from the notion that discrimination against whole groups that has been persistent, institutionalized, and long-term cannot be remedied by banning such actions. Although antidiscrimination legislation is essential, these policies emerge out of the recognition that such legislation may not be enough to create a work environment that provides a quality of opportunities for all, and may actually cement past inequalities.

Affirmative or positive action policies have two goals: (1) righting past wrongs—compensating groups that have been disadvantaged in the past with better opportunities in the present; and (2) achieving social goals of increasing the representation of traditionally disadvantaged groups in more lucrative jobs as well as management and leadership positions. The rationale behind these policies is that they redress past discrimination by giving preference in hiring and promotion to member of groups that have been discriminated against in the past. Considering that for a long time these groups have had limited access to education, high-paying and prestigious jobs, networks of influence, and promotion opportunities, they may continue to be deprived of these opportunities if not given a temporary emphasis until a more balanced representation can be achieved.

An opposing theory is that affirmative action policies are not necessary because employers should hire the best qualified candidates available without regard to cultural diversity. Under this theory, it is implied that cultural diversity does not contribute to organizational excellence. It also assumes that members of a minority community within the law enforcement agency's jurisdiction are not concerned with under-representation within the agency. It also assumes that the under-representation within the agency does not have an adverse effect on how minority members of the community are being treated by the officers. Opponents of this viewpoint believe that, under this philosophy, organizations would lose their competitive advantage if they do not utilize the wide range of skills and talents offered by women, members of minority groups, older adults, and people with disabilities. If law enforcement agencies continue in their failure to achieve cultural diversity, in particular, both their effectiveness and positive community relations will be diminished. Strictly following this logic, there is no need for any policies that encourage employers to give equal opportunities to all because it is in their own economic best interest and organizational effectiveness. The problem with the logic that a multicultural organization is performance-effective neutral, is that it assumes an employment decision will always be made objectively and be based on an employer's best interest. It disregards the fact that this behavior may be an embedded and deeply ingrained prejudicial perception that colors people's evaluations of other people's skills, abilities, and talents. In other words, if one is prejudice, say against older people, he or she will make a series of inaccurate assumptions concerning their qualifications, work ethic, technical skills, and values (Mor Barak, 2005).

In my opinion, affirmative action is not a policy that dictates an employer place an unqualified minority in a job. It is a policy that recognizes there are qualified minority candidates for a job and requires that an organization be pro-active in their recruitment and selection of these candidates. The great challenge of implementing an affirmative action plan is how to achieve the goal of increasing minority representation while maintaining organizational harmony. This is a process that must be managed in a systems approach and requires use of the five components previously stated, which are: Leadership, Planning and Research, Training and Education, Policy and Management Controls, Follow-up, and Feedback System. The length of time required to achieve workplace diversity must be taken into consideration by a law enforcement agency during the planning and preparation process. This affirmative action plan must indicate who, what, when, where, why, and how diversity is to be achieved.

References and Key Points on Creating A Multicultural Workforce

1. For the purpose of the book, diversity is defined as the variation of social and cultural identities among people existing together in a defined employment setting.
2. Achieving cultural or ethnic diversity is the primary challenge for law enforcement with regards to recruitment, selection, and retention, not so much other aspects of diversity.
3. The United States of America is the most culturally diverse nation in the world. Inscribed on the American currency is the phrase "E Pluribus Unum," which means "Out of many, one." It is the American belief that there is great strength in diversity.
4. The most fundamental purpose of law enforcement is to protect the constitutional rights of every individual.
5. Developing and implementing cultural diversity in an organization is a philosophy that must be leader-led. If the law enforcement CEO and the leadership team do not support this initiative, it is doomed to fail.
6. A tangible benchmark would be to achieve a composition of diversity in law enforcement agencies that is consistent with the ethnicity of the community.
7. This training plan should describe and explain the agency's affirmative action plan and include the strategies that shall be used for its achievement.

8. The chief must ensure that the organizational policies, procedures, rules, and regulations reflect the organization's philosophy and practices concerning human diversity. Employees and managers alike must be held accountable for compliance with these mandates.

9. The five strategy components of creating a multicultural organization are:

- Leadership
- Planning and Research
- Training and Education
- Policy and Management Controls
- Follow-up and Feedback System

10. The agency should compare and contrast the cultural diversity of the agency with that of its service population to develop its goals.

11. Training and education are required of all staff to create a multicultural agency.

12. The law enforcement agency's General Orders Manual should contain an overview of the agency's philosophy and standards for a multicultural environment.

13. All managers should be evaluated in part on their progress toward established diversity goals.

14. A follow-up and feedback system should be developed to measure the degree to which predetermined cultural diversity goals are being achieved and allow for corrective action.

15. Affirmative or positive action policies have two goals: (1) righting past wrongs—compensating groups that have been disadvantaged in the past with better opportunities in the present; and (2) achieving social goals of increasing the representation of traditionally disadvantaged groups in more lucrative jobs as well as management and leadership positions.

16. Affirmative action is not a policy that dictates an employer place an unqualified minority in a job. It is a policy that recognizes there are qualified minority candidates for a job and requires that an organization be pro-active in their recruitment and selection of these candidates.

References

Cox, Jr., T. (2001). *Creating the multicultural organization: A strategy for capturing the power of diversity.* Jossey-Bass, 2001, pp. 3 – 4.

Mor Barak, M. E. (2005). *Managing diversity - Toward a globally inclusive workplace.* California: Sage Publications, Inc.

Chapter 9

An Overview of the Law Enforcement Selection Process

It has been stated several times that the hiring of a law enforcement officer is the single most important functionf or any law enforcement agency. The quality of individuals hired will determine the quality of the agency.

Every law enforcement agency should conduct a review of the current police officer selection process from beginning-to-end to evaluate its effectiveness and efficiency. A systems approach should be taken to determine how and why you determine the suitability of potential law enforcement candidates. A law enforcement agency needs to understand why each component of the hiring process is used and what it is attempting to achieve regarding the screening of candidates. Each component of the selection process is different in its analysis of candidate suitability. However, collectively, all of the selection components of the hiring process both screen out undesirable traits and screen in desirable traits.

There are two general testing approaches with law enforcement selection tools; they are components of the selection process that either are screening-in or screening-out candidates. The screening-in approaches refers to those methods by which employers test applicants for competencies needed to perform well in an organization. Screening-in assessments include tests of knowledge, skill, and ability. Screening out assessments, in contrast, is the process of identifying vulnerabilities that would make a candidate a risk to the potential employer. Some examples of screening out assessments include background investigations, credit checks, drug screens, medical exams, and tests of psychopathology. It is important to understand that in the screening out process, the presence of a problem suggest a potential risk to the employer, but the absence of a problem does not imply a high level of future performance.

An agency should start at the very beginning with the job vacancy and map out the complete process through a final job offer. All the key stakeholders should meet to review and critique the hiring process. Key stakeholders include agency leadership, human resource managers, legal counsel, recruitment, officers, investigators, field training officers, and others directly involved with the hiring process. The stakeholders must be viewed as a valuable and integral part of improving the selection process.

During the review process, consider the following questions:

- Where does the process start and end?
- What processes are in place between the beginning and ending points?
- What is required in each phase of the process (i.e., POST or civil service)?
- How long do these steps take?
- Which steps can be modified, combined, eliminated, or outsourced?
- How is the job advertised and marketed?
- What is the perspective of candidates who have participated in the process?
- Does the process identify the best candidates in terms of skills, knowledge, and abilities desired by the agency (i.e., service-oriented versus adventure-oriented)?
- Does the process differentiate between candidates who are not trained, those who have graduated from a state peace officer standards and training (POST) certified academy, those who are laterals from other agencies, and those who work for the agency and are seeking to promote to a peace officer position?
- What is the current cost per candidate?
- Once a list is established, what rules apply as to how the names are certified for consideration, such as by individual score versus those ranked in broad bands?
- Is there a time limit for the agency executive to make a hiring decision?
- What responsibilities or roles are assigned to the law enforcement agency versus the Human Resource/Personnel Department?
- Who has ultimate responsibility for the hiring process? Is it one person?
- Do community representatives participate in any of the processes, such as the oral interview?

- Which aspects of the process are automated, if any?
- How does the current process compare with other agencies that are able to complete the process much faster or more effectively?
- Can steps on the process be automated? If so, can they be improved?

After this review is complete, there should be a good understanding of the process and where problems or opportunities exist. With this information in mind, an agency should establish some goals for improvement. What can be done with minimal time or resources? What is within the agency's power to change? What changes need the support of other stakeholders? List the goals in order of priority. There are three overall goals of your law enforcement officer hiring process. First, is to get the best available candidates. Second, is to ensure that the hiring process screens for the qualities and attributes that make a person effective in the job. Third, to complete the entire hiring process ideally in 90 days, but no more than 120 days.

The elimination of candidates from the selection process should be based on pre-established written standards of the law enforcement agency. Therefore, appropriate background removal standards for law enforcement officer candidates must be established. These background removal standards should include all of the following areas and describe the conditions that will eliminate a candidate from the application process:

1. Honesty/falsification
2. Family history
3. Employment
4. Military history
5. Traffic
6. Gambling
7. Criminal activity
8. Substance abuse
9. Applicant non-responsiveness

There should be a detailed description of the conditions on which an applicant is removed from the selection process based on not meeting the standards. A written document containing the background removal standards for law enforcement applicants, which is uniformly applied based on objective measures, is a must. This allows the agency to effectively respond to a legal challenge from an applicant in regards to being denied employment.

A law enforcement agency should review the Commission on Accreditation for Law Enforcement Agencies Standards Manual to ensure that all components of the hiring process comply with contemporary law enforcement standards. A law enforcement agency should develop a flexible profile of an effective police officer by identifying the "most viable candidates." The agency should identify the knowledge, skills, abilities, education, training, behaviors, and traits that make an effective officer. This identifies a target on which selection is based.

A law enforcement agency should attempt to do targeted selection to effectively recruit a law enforcement officer. The agency must know what it is looking for in quality candidates. Advertising alone is not effective recruitment. Successful recruitment must be efficient and effective. When efficiency and effectiveness are combined, the most appropriate selection tools are used for a smaller candidate pool.

A law enforcement agency should utilize a post-training academy. The post-training academy provides an opportunity to transition new recruits from the basic training academy to the field training officers program. The focus is on familiarization with key people within the agency's jurisdiction and key resources that recruits will interface with. It is an opportunity to provide an orientation to the administration of the government agency. New officers can become familiar with all the respective jurisdiction's buildings and respective departments. New officers should have the opportunity to visit with management personnel and meet members of the agency's command staff. New officers may be provided an opportunity to shadow dispatchers in the communications center. The post-training academy should be designed to provide any information that is not ideally suited for the basic training academy but would be advantageous to understand prior to beginning field training. It's a law enforcement best practice to have a post-training academy. This post-training academy addresses issues that help prepare the police recruit to begin the field training officers program.

An agency should design and implement at a minimum a 40-hour post-training academy that addresses key issues not well suited for either the basic training academy or the field officers training program.

The focus of this post training academy should be in the following key areas:

1. Meeting key individuals in the agency
2. Becoming familiar with key facilities within the jurisdiction
3. Familiarization with the key geographical areas of the jurisdiction
4. Briefings on any information or specialized topic not addressed in the basic-training academy

A Recommended Overview of the Law Enforcement Officer Selection Process

What are the key components of a selection process for hiring law enforcement officers? The recommended outline given here is designed to address the key areas of a selection process that both screen in and screen out the qualities and attributes required for a law enforcement officer. It is important to note that the quality of the process is dependent on the agency's prior planning and preparation along with its commitment to the process. The following are the recommended selection components for hiring a law enforcement officer in sequential order:

1. **Establish Law Enforcement Criteria for Officers**
    Identify the knowledge, skills, abilities, behaviors, and traits desired for the job through the use of a job analysis.

2. **Job Announcement**
    The public advertisement of the law enforcement job, which includes the job description, qualifications, and the complete hiring process with timeline from beginning to conclusion.

3. **Recruitment**
    The intentional process of seeking law enforcement candidates that match the predetermined qualities and attributes that contribute to job effectiveness.

4. **Written Examination**
    A written exam is a tool that can be used to determine whether or not candidates in the pool have the minimum

skills to perform functions required by the job. It is also used as a screening device, but not as a comprehensive method to determine qualifications.

5. **Physical Fitness Testing**
   It is important to law enforcement agencies that their officers develop and maintain a level of fitness that will enable them to carry out their tasks while minimizing the risk of injury and illness. Consequently, the agency should measure the level of fitness of its officer candidates to determine if they can perform essential job functions.

6. **Oral Interview**
   The oral interview should be utilized to establish whether the candidate possesses the criteria established for the law enforcement officer's job. It additionally evaluates the candidate's oral communications skills.

7. **Personal History Questionnaire**
   This questionnaire provides a profile of the candidate to assist in a thorough and complete background investigation of the candidate. This document provides a personal history profile of the candidate. The personal history profile listing the candidate's background assists in determining suitability for the job.

8. **Background Investigation**
   The investigation of the candidate's background should obtain information relating to the candidate's suitability or lack of suitability for law enforcement employment relative to his/her behavioral history and character.

9. **Polygraph**
   The polygraph is a scientific investigative analysis instrument utilized to determine the truthfulness of information provided in the application process or background investigation. A polygraph may assist in discovering pertinent information not reported in the application process.

10. **Entry-Level Assessment Center**

    The Entry-Level Assessment Center is a selection method that utilizes simulations to evaluate job-related knowledge, skills, abilities, behaviors, and traits. The primary focus of this method is to screen for strengths that will lead to job success as opposed to screening for deficiencies that may result in job failure.

11. **Psychological Examination**

    Psychological testing is utilized to identify candidates who are mentally and emotionally suited for law enforcement based on the job's qualifications, tasks, and environments. It should also identify those candidates not mentally and emotionally suited for law enforcement work.

12. **Medical Examination**

    The medical examination of law enforcement candidates should determine the overall health status of a law enforcement candidate. A medical examination may determine if a candidate is unable to perform an essential job function. Additionally, a medical examination should identify any pre-existing medical condition which may be aggravated during the basic academy or on the job.

13. **Recruit Training Academy**

    All candidates selected for hire by the agency should be required to successfully complete Basic Training Academy. This basic training school shall provide instruction on the requisite knowledge, skills, and abilities necessary to perform the basic functions of a law enforcement officer.

14. **Post-Training Academy**

    A Post-Training Academy will provide an orientation for law enforcement officers recently graduated from the Basic Training Academy on the job environment and community.

15. **Field Training Officer Program**

    Following the Post-Training Academy, new officers will ride with multiple field training officers over the course of several months to learn how to practically apply basic training knowledge on the job. Additionally, this program formally evaluates the candidate's ability to perform all essential job functions and job-related tasks. With the utilization of several training officers, the officer candidate's skills are enhanced by the mentoring process. This is the phase in which the new officer is successfully integrated into the job environment.

At the end of this chapter, there is a diagram, see Appendix 9-1, which provides a visual overview of the selection process recommended. When planning this selection process, an agency should establish a timetable for the completion of each component of the selection process.

A Systems Approach to Hiring

The Ohio Law Enforcement Foundation Entry-Level Assessment Center research grant identified 12 qualities desirable for law enforcement officers (review Chapter 1). These qualities are utilized in establishing the selection process components, including a recommended sequence of the hiring process. Each component in the hiring process evaluates specific criteria and must be developed and implemented based on its job relatedness. Each and every component in a hiring process is a test. Every test must contain two fundamental requirements.

1. *A test must be valid.* Validity means you are measuring what you should be measuring. The measurements are specifically related to the functions of the target job.

2. *A test must be reliable.* Reliability may be thought of as repeatability. You may repeat the process and obtain consistent results without bias towards any individuals or culture groups (adverse impact).

Each component in the hiring process should have the structural integrity to withstand a legal challenge. While these evaluation components recommended in the hiring process are not meant to be exhaustive, they are, however, designed to be a thorough process for hiring a law enforcement officer. The sequence of the selection process is flexible and should be designed based on the law enforcement agency's needs, cost effectiveness, resources and job environment. Each component should be identified in its recommended order with an overview of the qualities and/or traits it is measuring. More detailed information on each component is provided in the topical papers in this study. When law enforcement recruiters meet and get to know a potential law enforcement candidate, they are only observing the metaphoric "tip of the iceberg." Only 10 percent of an iceberg is observable above the surface. The remaining 90 percent is beneath the surface. Therefore, an informal pre-screening process with a candidate can reveal only approximately 10 percent of the individual. The other 90 percent may be discovered utilizing the selection process, understanding it is impossible to obtain 100 percent of the information concerning a candidate's qualifications. These selection components when used as a system provide a tremendous amount of information that can be used to make an effective hiring decision. See diagram in Appendix 9-2 at the end of this chapter.

Summary

The identification of selection criteria and resulting components of the selection process for law enforcement officer is critical to the success of the law enforcement agency's hiring process. The qualities and skills desired should be determined in advance of establishing the selection components along with the order of components in the hiring process. As a general rule, the employer should clearly indicate to the candidate(s) the requirements of the job and the process for filling the job, including the timetable, in advance of the selection process. Law enforcement agencies should reevaluate their hiring process to determine if the selection components they are using to identify qualified candidates for the agency are appropriate. The utilization of this hiring model should guide an agency in the development and implementation of a thorough and comprehensive hiring process. The end result is the hiring of law enforcement officers who provide a higher quality of law enforcement services to the community and participate in the accomplishment of agency goals.

Appendix 9-1

OFFICER SELECTION PROCESS

(AGENCY)_____

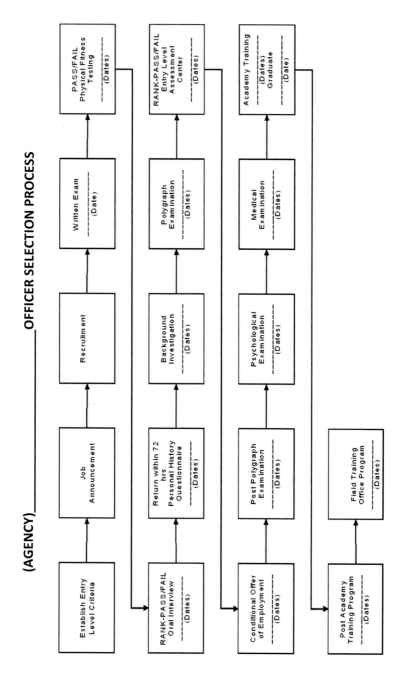

Appendix 9-2
The Iceberg Hiring Principle

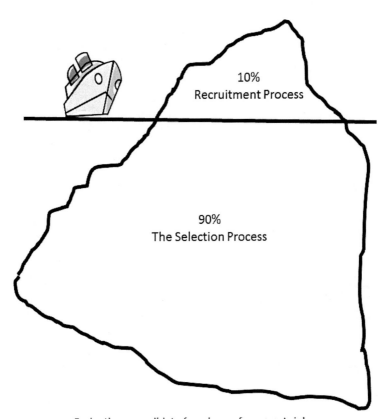

10%
Recruitment Process

90%
The Selection Process

Evaluating a candidate for a law enforcement job.

Recommendations and Key Points for the Law Enforcement Officer Selection Process

The following recommendations are made concerning selection criteria for law enforcement officers:

1. The hiring of a law enforcement office is the single most important function for any law enforcement agency.
2. The quality of individuals hired by a law enforcement agency will determine the quality of that agency.
3. If the people in your law enforcement agency are not competitive in the law enforcement profession, how can your agency be competitive in the law enforcement industry?
4. The first step in identifying the selection criteria for law enforcement officers at your agency is to identify your essential job functions, successful job related behaviors and traits.
5. The Ohio law enforcement research grant has identified 12 behaviors and traits desirable for law enforcement officers. These behaviors and traits are common for officers regardless of the type of law enforcement agency or its size.
6. To determine all the traits desirable for a law enforcement officer at a specific agency, a job analysis must be conducted.
7. A job analysis should include a review of the agency's mission statement; core values; agency goals; job description for the entry level officer; community needs and job environment.
8. The qualities for law enforcement officers have changed and will continue to change.
9. The changing job environment and candidate pool dictate that law enforcement agencies evaluate and modify their method of recruitment and selection of candidates on a periodic basis.
10. Every component of a selection process is a test. All tests must be both valid and reliable.
11. Sequence of the selection process is flexible, and should be designed based on the law enforcement agency's needs, cost effectiveness, resources, and job environment.

12. The qualities and skills desired should be determined in advance of establishing selection components and order of components in the hiring process.

13. As a general rule, the employer should clearly indicate to the applicants the requirements of the job, and the process of fulfilling the job in advance of beginning the process, including the timetable.

14. The selection components of a hiring process when used as a system provide a tremendous amount of information that can be used to make an effective hiring decision.

15. There are two general testing approaches with law enforcement selection tools they are components of the selection process that either are screening-in or screening-out candidates.

Chapter 10

Using a Written Examination

Why Written Exams Are Used

The most common instrument for initial screening of law enforcement entry-level candidates has been written examinations. Law enforcement agencies have been using written test since O. W. Wilson in his early police administration text discussed the need to administer intelligence tests, information tests, and psychological inventories as part of the selection process for law enforcement officers. Wilson indicated that police officers should be above average and possesses an intelligence quotient of at least 112 (Wilson, 1963). It is interesting to note that the original purpose of utilizing written examinations for law enforcement officers was to determine one's intelligence quotient relative to their suitability for law enforcement service.

Written exams remain a staple in the law enforcement selection process for law enforcement agencies large, medium, and small. As a law enforcement consultant, I have discovered that these exams are used without regard to what they are attempting to accomplish and how they complement other parts of the selection process. Administrators need to consider the characteristics of candidates who successfully complete these written exams and what the exams accomplish. Written exams are primarily used by law enforcement agencies to manage the applicant pool rather than to test the applicants' abilities or aptitudes to be police officers (Gaines, 1998). Both of these purposes are legitimate; however, the primary purpose should be to test the applicant's cognitive ability to serve as a law enforcement officer.

Employment Testing Legal Mandates

There are two significant legal issues that affect the use of written examinations. The first issue is related to the United States Supreme Court landmark decision rendered in the *Griggs v. Duke Power Co.* case in 1972. This case effectively made it illegal for unintentional discrimination to exist in employment testing procedures. It established the intent of Congress with regard to the Civil Rights Act of 1964 by stating that discriminatory effect (not intent) was the key consideration and that employment tests must be job related and consistent with business necessity. What is required is the removal of artificial, arbitrary, and unnecessary barriers to employment when such barriers discriminate on the basis of racial, sexual or other protected class. What Congress has in effect declared is that any tests used must measure the person for the job and not the person in the abstract. Following this decision, employers must now substantiate that testing procedures are valid when adverse impact occurs.

Adverse impact in employment occurs when employment practices that appear to be neutral have a discriminatory effect on a protected class. Under the Equal Employment Opportunity Commission (EEOC) Uniform Guidelines, adverse impact is defined as a substantially different rate of selection in hiring, promotion, or other employment decision that works to the disadvantage of members of a protected class. Adverse impact analysis involves comparing the selection rate for each group with the group that has the highest selection rate through the use of an impact ratio. The federal EEOC uniform guidelines include a rule of thumb for interpreting these ratios that is referred to as the "4/5ths" or "80 percent" rule. According to the 80 percent rule, adverse impact may exist if the selection rate for one group is less than 80 percent of the selection rate of the group with the highest selection rate.

The second legal issue that affects the use of written examinations is the Civil Rights Act of 1991. This act was passed in an attempted to eliminate self-imposed quota systems by specifically forbidding the use of any statistical methods or scoring adjustments to achieve racial or gender balance or parity. The Civil Rights Act of 1991 in effect prevented any agency for using any kind of score adjustment to achieve racial or gender parity. These two legal decisions create a delicate balancing act for hiring agencies to avoid civil rights litigation. Employment testing must not have an adverse impact on a protected class and yet agencies may not use any kind of statistical scoring adjustments to avoid adverse impact.

The Complex Nature of Law Enforcement Work

However, in today's job market, two important factors have made selection of personnel more complicated. First, the complex nature of the law enforcement job itself, which is continuing to increase in complexity. Second, the competitive nature of the job market, which has limited the pool of qualified candidates.

We ask the law enforcement officer of today to be a very talented person. First, we ask them to be a person of integrity, service, education, good human relation skills, and compassion. Law enforcement officers have to be able to write well and to observe and analyze facts rapidly, all the while ensuring that compassion and assistance are provided to victims. They have to work with increasingly technical equipment as necessary tools for addressing crime issues. Personal integrity is an essential element as well, along with an ability to interact with all aspects of the community. Once all of these qualities are found in a candidate, we ask them for an additional uncommon quality. They must be able to handle a life-and-death struggle on a moment's notice while using their good judgment to use minimum force. We not only ask for the physical ability and mental toughness to do this, but we ask for the common sense and good judgment under pressure. The fact is that no written test created can conclusively determine if many of these abilities are present in a candidate. The traditional written test was designed to measure cognitive ability, but typically showed adverse impact. Other written tests may be designed as personality measures, situational judgment tests, or emotional intelligence tests. Again, establishing validity (job-relatedness) may be difficult.

Planning Strategies for a Written Examination

How can we maximize the benefits of a written test, yet still overcome its limitations? The best answer is that the written testing process can be used in conjunction with other processes to ensure that qualified candidates are selected.

Steps to a successful written examination include:

- Understanding the job requirements through an accurate job task analysis
- Clearly defining your purpose and establishing realistic goals for the written test
- Selecting the most appropriate type of written test that best meets agency needs

- Allocating the funding necessary to complete the written testing process
- Ensuring that the written testing process fits in appropriately and efficiently with the rest of the selection process
- Provide sufficient time limits for individuals to take the exam
- Target the difficulty level to the mid-range of difficulty
- Consider the use of study guides and test preparation material

Strategies for Reducing Adverse Impact

The following are some strategies that a law enforcement agency may use to reduce adverse impact:

- Is there content that might be deemed to offensive to members of an Identifiable racial, cultural, ethnic, gender, religious, disability or age group?
- Does the test item perpetuate racial, cultural, ethnic, gender, religious, disability, or age related stereotypes?
- Will words or phrases used in the test item have different meanings for different subgroups?

Job Task Analysis

The job task analysis is conducted in such a way that the agency is looking for the right things in a candidate. Each agency's "ideal candidate" is different based on the actual tasks that will be done once the officer is in the position. For example, the function of a deputy sheriff, state patrol trooper, and municipal officer are clearly different. Additionally, the demographics of each individual jurisdiction, along with the culture of the individual agency, vary greatly.

This accurate assessment of the job tasks required is an important first step. The Commission on Accreditation for Law Enforcement Agencies, Inc. (CALEA) has identified the important elements of a valid job task analysis. At a minimum, a job task analysis must include detailed work behaviors (duties, responsibilities, functions, and tasks), the frequency with which the various tasks are performed, and the criticality (importance) of each task. The job task analysis attempts to identify the job-related skills, knowledge, and abilities so that the selection process can be designed to be content valid.

A job task analysis is conducted by examining the existing position for which you are testing; questionnaires and interviews with officers currently in the position for which candidates will be tested are essential elements of the process. Input from supervisors, administrators from the governmental entity, and personnel department representatives should also be included to gain the necessary perspective of the total environment for the job. More extensive information on the job task analysis process is provided in Chapter 2 of this book.

Goals of the Testing Process

The job task analysis is then used to assist in defining agency testing goals. What are the goals of your written test? Is it simply to reduce the numbers to a manageable level? If this is the only goal, the result is likely to be that a significant number of unqualified candidates will get through the process, causing disruption to the agency in a number of ways. As previously stated the primary goal of a written exam is ensure the candidates have the intellectual capability to perform the job.

One of the significant advantages of a written test is evident, the ability to test large numbers of candidates in an objective, legally defensible way at low cost. By reducing the number of potential candidates to a smaller number, agency resources are conserved in all of the ensuing activities such as conducting interviews, background investigations, polygraph testing, psychological examinations, medical examinations, and so on.

It is helpful to define what level of written expertise is required. Does the agency simply want an officer who can fill out a report? Are there other more complex expectations than written projects and presentations to be done? With clear expectations set, the effective selection of a written examination can be made. In addition, should the exam concern itself only with knowledge, or are attitudinal considerations part of the goal in the written test? These questions must be asked before a particular exam is chosen.

Once the goals based on your task analysis are established, the evaluation of various written exams to meet your needs can begin.

In choosing which specific exam to use, ask the following questions:

- **How competent is your particular selection pool?**
  If you have a pool of candidates of the highest quality, the test should be more difficult to differentiate between candidates. If the candidate pool is small and relatively less educated, a different, less-stringent test might be required to ensure that qualified candidates receive passing scores.

- **Do your goals include simply measuring technical ability to perform the job, or do you wish to begin screening for other factors?**
  Most standardized tests may meet the basic needs, although they rarely measure writing ability or which candidates may be most suitable. If these additional qualities are desired at the written testing level, there are stamina-based tests that may provide them.

- **What is the demonstrated validity of the test?**
  Can the company provide a defensible validity document that can aid in protecting your agency in case of later litigation? The testing process must be demonstrably job related and be free of adverse impact.

- **Does the test lend itself to being administered, scored, evaluated and interpreted in an accurate and equitable manner?**
  Ensuring that these factors are considered adds to the confidence you can have that the written test will provide viable candidates.

- **What service will the testing company provide if the test is challenged?**
  "Service after the sale" is important when the inevitable challenges occur.

The specific test type, difficulty level, and testing company are selected based on the answers to these questions.

The traditional, multiple-choice, entry-level tests were based on cognitive ability. However, this test type, like all others, needs to be concerned about adverse impact. As leaders in the law enforcement field searched for better testing methods, alternative processes such as personality-based tests, biographical data testing (objectively scored), and situational judgment tests have emerged.

Test Funding Issues

Take a realistic view of your written testing costs. A "canned" test for the written segment may meet all of your agency needs at a minimal cost as long as it is validated for your target job. However, if you wish to measure more complicated factors or your job task analysis indicates that more specialized skills are necessary, the cost may go much higher. If a test is individually designed for a specific agency, costs can rise dramatically due to the intensive man hours required for development.

Contact as many companies as you can to compare how their products fit the needs your agency has identified. Be sure that you are comparing like products when you compare price. Make contact with local and national law enforcement organizations and other agencies as you gather information. Law enforcement associations may provide vendor recommendations for written exams. Do not commit to any testing process until you are positive that funding is available in your agency.

Fitting In With the Overall Selection Process

The written test you choose should be compatible with the other steps in your selection process. If, for example, you intend to use an Entry-Level Assessment Center process later that includes written scenarios, narrative tests may not be needed in this early stage. If a high proportion of the candidates continue on to the next phase with the written test used only as a pass or fail, minimum qualifications test, then the written test may not need to be as extensive.

Once again my belief is that the most appropriate function of the written test is to determine whether or not the candidate has the minimum intellectual ability to perform the functions required by the job. Once this is assessed then other knowledge, skills, abilities, behaviors, and traits can be more accurately measured by other components of the selection process. Therefore it is my bias that based on this consideration, along with the issue-adverse impact, that pass-fail written examination method be utilized. I believe a rank-order written exam method locks an agency into a rank-order screening process, which otherwise has no relationship to the quality of the applicants. Here is another problem posed by written exam rank-order method. Hypothetically let's imagine there are only 100 people taking a law enforcement exam, and they are all of equal intelligence with ten minorities in the group. What are the ten minorities chances of being in the top 10 or 20 percent? They are less than the majority; and in this example, it is not based on intelligence but because of the reduced number of minorities in the pool. This pass-fail system allows an agency to screen all the candidates that demonstrate intellectual job-related fitness. Of course, for larger agencies or agencies with a large candidate pool another or multiple other selection components must serve the dual purpose of reducing the candidate pool.

Summary

Written testing processes are valuable tools that can be used to help select the most viable candidates. The written test is best used as a very early screening device, not an "end-all" to establish a list for hiring.

It is extremely important for an agency to carefully evaluate their needs so that the best written testing mechanism can be chosen. The written testing process should be based on the actual work that the candidate will be expected to do, and specifically address agency goals. The testing type and method should be selected after considering the job task analysis and what level of resources are available, as well as be defensible from a valid and non-discriminatory content basis.

Recommendations and Key Points for Developing a Written Examination

The following recommendations are made concerning the written examination process.

1. Understand the target job prior to selecting a written test through an accurate job task analysis.
2. The most common instrument for initial screening of law enforcement entry level candidates has been written examinations.
3. Written exams it appears are primarily used by law enforcement agencies to manage the applicant pool rather than test the applicant's abilities or aptitudes to be police officers. Both of these purposes are legitimate; however, the primary purpose should be to test the applicant's cognitive ability to serve as a law enforcement officer.
4. There are two significant legal issues that affect the use of written examinations. The first issue is related to the United States Supreme Court landmark decision, rendered in the *Griggs v. Duke Power Co.* case in 1972. This case effectively made it illegal for unintentional discrimination to exist in employment testing procedures.
5. The second legal issue that affects the use of written examinations is the Civil Rights Act of 1991. This act was passed to eliminate self-imposed quota systems by specifically forbidding the use of any statistical methods or scoring adjustments to achieve racial or gender balance or parity.
6. Clearly define the purpose and realistic goals for your written test.
7. Select the most appropriate type of written test that best meets the law enforcement agency's needs.
8. Allocate the funding necessary to complete the written testing process.
9. Insure that the written test fits in appropriately and efficiently with the rest of the selection process.
10. Prior to selecting a written test, determine how competent your particular selection pool of candidates is.
11. Contact as many companies as you can to compare how their products fit the needs your agency has identified.

12. Law enforcement associations may provide vendor recommendations for written exams.
13. What is the demonstrated validity of your written test?
14. Can the testing company you hire provide a defensible, valid document that can aid in testing your agency in case of litigation?
15. Ensure that your written test is job related and free of adverse impact.
16. Determine in advance what services the testing service agency provides if the test is challenged.

References

Age Discrimination in Employment Act of 1967.

Americans with Disabilities Act of 1990.

Civil Rights Act of 1991

Commission on Accreditation for Law Enforcement Agencies Standard Manual, Fifth Edition, Revised.

Gaines, L., & Falkenberg, S. (1998). An evaluation of the written selection test: Effectiveness and alternatives. Journal of Criminal Justice (Vol. 26, No. 3, pp.175 – 183).

Griggs v. Duke Power Co., 401 U.S. 424. Retrieved from Cornell University Law School, Legal Information Institute website.

Oliver, P., et. al. (2001). *The Complete Guide to Hiring Law Enforcement Officers: Based on a Research Study of the Entry Level Assessment Center Method.* The Law Enforcement Foundation, Inc.: Columbus, OH.

Uniform Guidelines on Employee Selection Procedures of 1978.

Wilson, O. W. (1963). Police administration. New York: McGraw-Hill Book Co.

Chapter 11

Physical Fitness Testing

Physical Fitness Testing Is a Confusing and Complex Issue

Physical fitness testing is the most challenging area to address in a law enforcement selection process. There is much information concerning the viability of agility testing for entry-level candidates in law enforcement. There is much confusion about what to do and how to do it. Additionally, there is much disagreement and confusion regarding gender- and age-based fitness norms for law enforcement officer applicants. There are certainly dangers and risks associated with law enforcement work. Many studies on the topic of the dangers associated with the law enforcement profession have come to the conclusion that certain tasks of the job are dangerous (Henson, 2003). The dangers of the profession range from homicides and assaults, which are most serious and less frequent, to injuries, most of which result from automobile crashes. To accurately analyze the job in relation to physical fitness, one must research the severity, frequency, and job tasks with or without the potential for danger and its direct relationship to physical fitness to accomplish. Law enforcement is generally sedentary in nature; however, there are rare times when a maximum effort must be exerted. The validation of a physical agility test for law enforcement officers is difficult at best. The challenge lies in achieving agreement in the physical capabilities that should be tested and the standards that should be used to evaluate those physical capabilities. To comply with current legislation fitness test standards and programs must be job related and scientifically valid.

Regardless of the difficulty of validating a physical fitness test, it is important to law enforcement agencies for officers to maintain a level of physical fitness that enables them to carry out any tasks they may be called upon to perform, while minimizing the risk of injury and illness. Ideally the requirement of a physical agility test should be combined with a department's commitment to physical fitness for its incumbent officers. The physical fitness test is based on the requirement of business necessity. If there is not a fitness standard for the agency's officers in-service then the argument of it being an essential job function is nullified. There can be a fitness evaluation component to a program alone, or with components to encourage law enforcement personnel to maintain a fit, healthy lifestyle (wellness program).

Why Utilize Fitness Exams

In many occupations, the daily level of physical exertion is predictable, but not so in law enforcement. For extended periods of time, an officer may operate at a minimal level of physical activity and then be called on to exert a critical amount of physical and mental energy. Consequently, it is incumbent on each officer to ensure he or she is physically fit and able to endure physical and mental abuse, because his or her very survival may someday depend upon it. A physical fitness test measures the "physical ability" of a candidate's capability to perform strenuous job tasks.

Physical fitness is a proven component of officer readiness and one of the law enforcement officer's main field encounter survival tools. Many law enforcement academies have conducted physical fitness training and graduates leave their academy physically fit. In most cases, officers are then left on their own to maintain their fitness without the support of the agency. There is no across-the-board standard in law enforcement for fitness. Some agencies test at entry alone, while others are incorporating some form of fitness plan with current employees.

Hoffman (1993) reports on the well-known 1977 Comprehensive Fitness Study by the Cooper Institute of Aerobics Research by Tom Collingwood, Ph.D., where test group officers tested lower on fitness and higher on heart disease factors, as compared to the general population. The data generated by the institute has repeatedly indicated the need for law enforcement officers to maintain their physical fitness throughout their career, not only for job performance, but also to minimize disease and poor health risk profiles.

Joint studies by the Cooper Institute and the International Association of Chiefs of Police resulted in specific guidelines for law enforcement fitness programs. Cooper Institute standards are generally the most used in law enforcement fitness programs. The National Advisory Commission of Criminal Justice Standards and Goals has also recommended that law enforcement agencies establish fitness standards. Hoffman also cites Frank J. Landy,

Pennsylvania State University psychologist, who has studied retired officers and believes physical fitness and mental acuity are much better predictors of a law enforcement officer's effectiveness than is his age. FBI studies indicate the three key factors to law enforcement officer's survival other than his age. The three key factors to law enforcement survival of a shooting incident are: (1) physical fitness, (2) weapons knowledge, and (3) the will to survive.

Areas of concern in the application of physical tests are primarily legal issues and adverse impact. Potential obstacles to conducting physical tests are (1) budget constraints, (2) the application of industrial insurance coverage, and (3) law enforcement union resistance.

The Cooper Institute gives the following reasons that law enforcement agencies should be concerned with the fitness of their officers:

- It relates to the ability of the officers to perform essential functions of the job.
- It relates to minimizing the risk of excessive force situations.
- It relates to minimizing the known health risks associated with the public safety job.
- It relates to meeting many legal requirements to avoid litigation and have a defensible position if challenged in court.

Basic Physical Fitness Components That May Be Measured

In an article for *Police Chief* magazine, Dr. Thomas R. Collingwood, et al., determined that it is possible to document that specific fitness areas underlie task performance. Areas such as aerobic and anaerobic power, strength, flexibility, explosive power, and agility are related to performance in the law enforcement officer jog. This conclusion is supported by data collected over 15 years from 34 physical performance standards validation studies performed on more than 5,500 incumbent officers representing 75 federal, state, and local law enforcement agencies. These officer samples were stratified by gender and age and they were randomly selected. Due to the size of the sample, the study team believe the results can be applicable to law enforcement officers in general. (Collingwood, Hoffman, & Smith, 2004)

These 34 physical fitness standards validation studies data indicate that certain physical fitness areas are the underlying and predictive factors or physical abilities that determine a law enforcement officer's capabilities to perform essential physical tasks.

These factors are identified as follows:

- Aerobic power as measured by the 1.5-mile run
- Anaerobic power as measured by the 300-meter run
- Upper-body absolute strength as measured by the 1RM bench press
- Upper-body muscular endurance as measured by the push-up test
- Abdominal muscular endurance as measured by the one-minute sit-up test
- Explosive power as measured by the vertical jump
- Agility as measured by the Illinois agility run

Collingwood et al., indicated that these findings were straightforward which are:

- Test for these areas to ensure that applicants, academy recruits, and incumbents have the physical abilities to perform the essential physical tasks of the job.
- Develop performance standards in these areas for utilization with applicants, academy recruits, and incumbents.
- Provide training programs that ensure that law enforcement recruits and incumbents have the skills and knowledge to maintain personal conditioning programs throughout their career.

Physical fitness may involve a variety of measures. It may include levels of muscular strength, cardiovascular endurance, muscle tone, heart action, or response to activity.

The Fitness Model of physical testing designed by the Cooper Institute for Aerobics Research is used by hundreds of public safety agencies across the United States. The premise for the test is that being physically fit is a good predictor of job success for law enforcement and fire department personnel.

Examples of physical fitness testing are:

- **Cardiovascular Test**
  This may include a one or one-half mile run or a three-mile walking test to measure cardiovascular-respiratory endurance. These tests are conducted with the participants running/walking as fast as they can. If walking is required (and not running) the participant must keep one foot in contact with the ground during the entire test.
- **Dynamic Strength**
  This component measures sit-ups or push-ups. Personnel are evaluated on the number they can complete in a set time, such as one minute. Dynamic strength or endurance is measured with a minimum passing number.
- **Absolute Strength**
  This measures maximum body strength through bench presses or leg presses. The participant's maximum body strength is measured after a warm-up exercise with a maximum number of attempts allowed (for example, three). The bench press is conducted on a Universal weight machine with the individual pressing the maximum of weight at one time. The minimum amount of weight needed to pass is based on a ratio of weight pressed to body weight. The leg press is also on a Universal weight machine, with the participant pressing the maximum amount of weight one time. The required weight is also determined by a weight ratio.

Physical fitness testing must be related to essential job functions. Candidates should be notified in advance that a physical fitness test is part of the selection process. If a candidate has an issue concerning the test, he or she should put the concern in writing. All issues concerning physical fitness testing will be handled on a case-by-case basis. An agency may decide to administer medical screening prior to a physical test. However, a conditional offer of employment must be made. Candidates for employment may undergo a full medical examination after a conditional offer of employment. Current employees may be given a prescreening test as an update, with an exam administered if there are medical concerns regarding a participant.

Some prescreening tests could include:

- Blood pressure
- Resting heart rate
- Accelerated heart rate (after a three-minute step test)
- Body composition
- Flexibility (sit and reach)
- Nutrition assessment

What Constitutes Valid and Defensible Fitness Examinations

Validity and job relatedness are the two primary requirements of fitness tests. Validity is a vital facet in pre-employment testing, especially when there are potential equal employment liabilities. Arvey, Landon, Nutting and Maxwell (1992) noted research that some tests were likely to adversely affect females. They discussed Hogan's review of 14 studies where correlations between various physical ability tests and some kind of criterion measure such as training time, job tenure, ratings of job performance, and work sample performance were reported. In their own study, the group found evidence for the construct validity of a set of physical ability test events that could be used in selecting law enforcement officers. The evidence suggested that two constructs, strength and endurance, underlie both performance on the tests and performance on the job, and therefore satisfy the linkage requirements for construct validity in The Uniform Guidelines on Employee Selection Procedures of 1978.

For job relatedness to be accepted for a standard, a validation needs to be conducted. As described by Collingwood, a test is valid if it measures a dimension or factor that has bearing on the individual's capability to perform the job. He reviewed the guidelines for validation of standards defined by the EEOC in The Uniform Guidelines on Employee Selection Procedures, which define three validation strategies that are acceptable for demonstrating the job relatedness of a given standard: content, construct, and criterion validation. Content validity refers to the content (properties) measured by a test as being the same as the properties of a specific job task or function. Tests that are content valid are usually task simulation ability tests. Construct validity refers to the test's ability to measure an underlying factor or dimension that is a characteristic of an officer's ability to perform many job tasks. In fitness testing, upper body strength may be measured as a factor in ability to perform job tasks like use of force and lifting. Criterion validity refers to a test measuring a dimension that is predictive of, or correlated with, criterion performance of job tasks. Aerobic power could predict an officer's ability to complete a pursuit. Construct validation was determined to be a preferred method of validation of physical ability testing by Collingwood, and in 1992 by Arvey, Nutting, and Landon.

Legal Requirements Regarding Tests

Tests cannot be discriminatory against protected classes (females, minorities, handicapped, or older adults). The Civil Rights Acts of 1964 and 1991, the Americans with Disabilities Act and the Age Discrimination in Employment Act provide protection to individuals in those classes. The Americans with Disabilities Act (ADA) and the 1991 Civil Rights Act made it illegal to use different standards for hiring men and women. The ADA demonstrates potential problems in the use of physical ability testing. The ADA requires that employers selecting from applicants for a position focus on whether the applicant can perform the essential functions of the job. The Equal Employment Opportunity Commission ADA technical assistance manual states that an employer should determine if the individual can perform the essential functions of the job, with or without reasonable accommodation.

The application of physical ability testing in public safety can discriminate, if job relatedness is recognized and well documented. The use of physical fitness testing needs to identify those who can do the job and those who are unable to do the job.

Biddle & Sill (1999) discussed the potential legal challenges to physical testing in the public sector. Many agencies have focused on the development, validation and use of physical ability tests. They found the use just as important as the development and validation, as a valid test may still be vulnerable in a court case, even though appropriately developed and validated.

Rating and Ranking Fitness Scores

A key consideration in physical ability testing is setting pass/fail cutoffs that accurately reflect the physical ability levels required for successful job performance. Practices such as pass/fail cutoffs, top-down ranking, banding and grouping passing applicants, and weighting or combining physical ability test results with other pre-employment tests are used by public agencies.

The use of physical ability tests is just as important, if not more so, than the soundness of the validity by which they are constructed, Biddle and Sill found. Determining a pass/fail cutoff should be set between selecting the best qualified physical performers and the selection of the level that represents the true physical ability needed for satisfactory job performance.

Top-down ranking is not considered the best way to use physical ability test scores. Adverse impact, strict scrutiny by the courts, and the fact that tests are simulations and somewhat limited in their ability to discern proportionate job performance differences should discourage agencies from rank ordering on physical ability tests. Biddle and Sill stated that banding was a better approach, as it displays the benefit of rank ordering that minimizes adverse impact.

Hogan and Quigley reported in 1986 that the area of assessing physical standards was particularly challenging, because many standards result in adverse impact. They then recommended that the measurement base of physical employment tests continue to expand and new measures be developed with high validity coefficients and with less adverse impact. Hogan and Quigley found the use of valid selection procedures for physically demanding jobs to be justified both scientifically and legally. They also predicted that the tension created by the promise of equality of opportunity and the expectation of equality of outcome will exist for some time. Their prediction continues today.

The Cooper Institute recommends the use of absolute standards of single cutoffs. However, because this recommendation may adversely impact women to meet the same standard for the same job as males, it is important that if gender-based standards are developed regarding physical strength and agility, the standards be validated and criterion validity be used to predict who can or cannot perform the job. This is a controversial area and each agency should seek legal advice before establishing standards.

The institute describes three methods that agencies have used in applying standards: (1) a construct/criterion validation study for an individual agency, (2) a transferability study, and (3) applying another agency's absolute standard. A construct/criterion validation study for that individual agency is the most defensible. Study results should show which cutoffs should be the job standard. A second method is a transferability study. Using this approach, an agency demonstrates its strong similarity to another agency that has validated standards. A commonality analysis is used in this method. A third approach is to apply another agency's absolute standard. This is a less defensible approach than the previous two but is considered better than using percentile rankings of age and gender norms, which are not designed from validation studies.

In the 1990s some law enforcement agencies modified their fitness standards due to the law changes and legal challenges. They found their previous standards outdated. In requiring their job descriptions to conform to federal law, measurements used for applicants were deemed valid for veteran officers, with some age allowances. Therefore, the essential job functions listed on the position job description could be measured by the same instrument. They moved from a strength/endurance-based program to essential function events, which included backyard pursuit, stretcher carry, body drag, and 300-yard sprint events.

Adverse impact can be shown if less that 80 percent of a protected class of employees (or potential employees) passed a given standard at the pass rate of the majority. A protected class was defined in terms of ethnicity (Black, Hispanic, Native American, etc.) and gender (female). The Age Discrimination in Employment Act (ADEA) established in 1978 adds a protected class of elderly. Adverse impact has brought court review of physical ability pre-employment testing for possible discrimination. If adverse impact is identified, the physical ability test can be maintained only if it is shown to be job related. This job relatedness component is also reiterated through the ADA and Civil Rights Act of 1991.

Collingwood asserts that physical tests such as aerobic endurance, anaerobic power, absolute strength, dynamic strength, body composition, and flexibility demonstrate the type of valid data necessary to document them as job related. The defensibility of ability tests must be based on job relatedness data and precedence, not just opinion. Collingwood emphasizes that it is data support for the job relatedness of physical fitness and the validity of specific physical tests, and courts have shown an acceptance of physical fitness and physical ability tests as being job related and valid. Therefore, Collingwood defends the justification for physical ability tests.

In a review of the effects of preparing for physical ability tests shows methods for reducing potential adverse impact. Hogan and Quigley found that upper body strength and muscular endurance of non-athletic females could be enhanced by calisthenics training, with average gains from 30 percent to 50 percent. They also noted that test preparation activities are useful, such as test tryouts. They believe test tryouts have positive results for both applicants and employers.

Test tryouts can be through:

- The opportunity to view demonstrations and to take tryout tests provides a realistic job preview.
- Potentially qualified individuals can maximize their test performance by assessing their strengths and weaknesses in the tryout sessions and then by training in areas of deficiency.
- When candidates are given the opportunity to observe proper test-taking strategies, and practice those strategies or the ones that work best for them, criticisms of technique biased tests can be minimized.

In 1999, De Corte suggested the use of a generally applicable procedure of obtaining predictor composites so the average quality of the composite-selected employees is minimized, the intended selection rate was achieved, and adverse impact ratio remained within acceptable bounds. Predictor composites could be implemented that comply with the Equal Employment Opportunity Commission rule that adverse impact is present if the selection ratio for the minority group is less than four-fifths of the selection ratio or the majority group.

Applicable Results of a National Study

In an article for *Police Chief Magazine,* Thomas Collingwood et al. (2004) indicated that he and his co-authors have been involved for 30 years on establishing physical fitness programs and standards in hundreds of municipal, state, and federal law-enforcement agencies. The question being studied was how to prove that being physically fit is job-related? Using data collected during a 15 year period the study team concluded that it is now possible to document fitness areas such as aerobic and anaerobic power, strength, flexibility, explosive power, and agility in relation to specific task performance. They indicated their analysis conclusions are supported by data collected from 34 physical performance standards validation studies performed on more than 5,500 incumbent officers representing 75 state, federal, and local law enforcement agencies. The officer samples used in this study from each agency were stratified by age and gender, and selected randomly. They believed based on the size of the sample, that the results can be generalized as being applicable to law enforcement officers in general.

The results obtained from the 34 physical fitness standards validation studies claim that certain physical fitness areas are the underlying and predictive factors or physical abilities that determine a law enforcement officer's is capabilities to perform essential physical tasks. These factors are identified along with their findings on page 100 of this chapter.

Physical Fitness Policy Checklist

The Cooper Institute provides a top ten checklist for administrators implementing physical fitness testing.

1. Are the purposes and goals clearly defined?
2. Is the rationale behind the purposes and goals clearly defined?
3. Has the job-related validity for the test, standards, and programs been demonstrated and documented?
4. Are the personnel subject to the policies and programs identified from the top down?
5. Are the personnel responsible for implementing and supervising the program identified?

6. Are the primary fitness components of the program clearly identified and explained?
7. Are the operational components of the program clearly defined and explained?
8. Is the implementation process with timelines defined?
9. Are the organization's responsibilities specified?
10. Are the individual officer's responsibilities defined?

Summary

While physical ability testing is a more contemporary issue in law enforcement selection, there is more yet to be discovered, tested, and challenged. Researchers will strive for more thorough methods to measure physical ability and improvement of such tests. A number of law enforcement agencies are moving to a job-related abilities test instead of a physical agility test. Progressive agencies will continue to implement tests devised to select the most qualified individuals without the potential for adverse impact. Any physical fitness test developed should be reviewed by personnel experts and the government agency's legal counsel prior to implementation.

Recommendations and Key Points for Physical Fitness Testing

The following recommendations are made concerning physical fitness testing for law enforcement candidates:

1. It is important to law enforcement agencies for officers to maintain a level of physical fitness that enables them to perform any tasks required, while minimizing the risk of injury and illness.
2. Physical fitness is a proven component of law enforcement readiness and an important field survival tool.
3. A study at the Cooper Institute of Aerobics Research has indicated the need for officers to maintain a fitness lifestyle for job performance and reduced health risks.
4. The Cooper Institute standards are the most used in law enforcement fitness testing.
5. The National Advisory Commission of Criminal Justice Standards and Goals has recommended law enforcement agencies establish fitness standards.

6. FBI studies indicate the three key factors to law enforcement survival of a shooting incident are: (1) physical fitness, (2) weapons knowledge, and (3) the will to survive.
7. The primary areas of concern in developing and implementing physical fitness tests are: (1) legal issues, particularly adverse impact, (2) budget constraints, (3) the application of insurance coverage, and (3) law enforcement union resistance.
8. Validity and job relatedness are the two primary requirements of fitness testing.
9. An employer should determine if a candidate can perform the essential functions of the job with or without reasonable accommodation.
10. The application of physical ability testing in public safety can discriminate if job relatedness is recognized and well documented. Testing needs to identify those who can do the job and those unable to do the job.
11. It is recommended to use a pass/fail cutoff score set between selecting the best qualified performers and the selection of the level that represents the true physical ability needed for satisfactory job performance.
12. Adverse impact can be shown if less than 80 percent of a protected class of employees or potential employees passed a given standard at the pass rate of the majority.
13. The Cooper Institute provides a top ten checklist for administrators implementing physical fitness testing.
14. Any physical fitness test developed should be reviewed by personnel experts and the government agency's legal counsel prior to implementation.

References

Americans with Disabilities Act of 1990.

Age Discrimination in Employment Act of 1967.

Arvey, R.D., Nutting, S.N., & Landon, T. (1992). Validation strategies for physical ability testing in police and fire settings. *Public Personnel Management, Vol. 21(3)*, p. 301-312.

Arvey, R.D., Landon, T.E, Nutting, S.M., &Maxwell, S.E. Development of physical ability tests for police officers: A construct validation approach. *Journal of Applied Psychology, Vol. 77(6)*, p. 996-1009.

Biddle, D. & Sill, N.S. (1999). Protective service physical ability tests: Establishing pass/fail, ranking and banding procedures. *Public Personnel Management, Vol. 28(2)*, p. 217-225.

Collingwood, T.R. (1999). Physical fitness standards: Measuring job relatedness. *Journal of Applied Psychology, Vol. 84 (5)*, p. 695-702.

Collingwood, T.R., Hoffman, R., Smith, J. (2004). Underlying physical fitness factors for performing police officer physical tasks. *The Police Chief.* Vol. 72, No. 3. International Association of Chiefs of Police, Alexandria, VA.

The Cooper Institute, Law Enforcement/Public Safety fitness recommendations, 2010.

De Corte, W. (1999). Weighing job performance predictors to both maximize the quality of the selected workforce and control the level of adverse impact. *Journal of Applied Psychology, Vol. 84(5)*, p. 695-702.

Henson, Henry P. "Law enforcement officers wanted good people for a thankless job." *FBI Law Enforcement Bulletin*, v. 72 issue 4, 2003, p. 22-23.

Hoffman, A. (1993). Add muscle to your fitness programs. *Law Enforcement Technology*, p. 24-27.

Hogan, J. & Quigley, A.M. (1994). Effects of preparing for physical ability tests. *Public Personnel Management, Vol. 23(1)*, p. 85-104.

Hogan, J. & Quigley, A.M. (1986). Physical standards for employment and the courts. *American Psychologist, Vol. 41(11)*, pp. 1193-1217.

Simpson, L.D. (1995). A struggle to achieve fitness. *Law and Order*, p.16.

Chapter 12

Conducting Oral Interviews

Types of Interview Questions

There are two basic types of questions that may be asked of job candidates in an interview setting. One type of question is a theoretical question. In this type of question, we ask a candidate what they would do in a particular work situation, or how they might handle a job-related issue. The response given is based on what they may or may not actually do in that particular situation. The questions are theoretical in the sense that the candidates are giving a hypothetical response to a hypothetical question. The candidate's immediate mental response is probably what they (the potential employer) are looking for as the correct answer. The answer given will likely not be their actual response if they were faced with the same challenge in a real-life situation. The deficiency of this type of question is that it does provide the employer with an accurate profile of the candidate.

The second type of question is a behavioral-based interview question. In this type of question a candidate is asked how they have demonstrated a job-related skill or behavior in the past and to provide a specific example while indicating the outcome of their actions. In this type of question the candidate must not just think of a hypothetical response but must state what they actually did in a given situation and explain the outcome. This is more effective because it tells the prospective employer how and why the candidate actually makes the decision and how effective it is. If you gathered all the psychologists, sociologists, and human resource experts of the world and asked them about many topics, they would probably disagree on all of the topics except one. The one topic they would all be in unanimous agreement is this: the best indicator of future performance is past and current performance. Stated another way: the best indicator of what someone will do is what they have done. If someone does not have a history of service or integrity, you have no reasonable expectation of that behavior when they begin employment with your organization. This is not to suggest that it is impossible for the person to exhibit that behavior. It just validates that if there is no history of the behavior, you cannot reasonably expect a future demonstration of it.

Conduct a Behavioral-based Job Interview

Behavioral-based oral interviews are recommended for all law enforcement officer candidates. Interview questions must be based on job-related knowledge, skills, abilities, behaviors, and traits.

The following principles should be followed when conducting behavioral-based interviews.

• Behavioral-based interviews function on the understanding that past performance is the best indicator of future performance.

• The behavioral-based interview will compare the candidate's past performance with the criteria identified for job success and assist in determining if a candidate has the requisite skills and abilities.

• All interview questions must be job-related and valid.

• Training is required for the individual developing job-related questions and participating in an oral interview board.

• All persons evaluating the interviewee should be provided with information on properly evaluating the candidate's responses in comparison to effective job-related behaviors.

• Behavioral-based interview questions should be modified or updated as knowledge, skills, abilities, behaviors, and traits for the job changes.

• Prior to conducting an interview questions should be developed based on a job analysis and must be standardized for all candidates.

An essential purpose of any oral interview is to evaluate the candidate's suitability for the target job. This can only be done effectively if the interview questions are both job-related and reliable.

In the human relations profession, behavioral-based interview questions are considered to be a more valid and reliable method for conducting job interviews. Due to the high degree of validity, these questions are able to withstand a potential challenge by a candidate.

A Behavioral-based Interview System

It may be argued that the oral interview can provide the most accurate and comprehensive information on a job candidate's ability to do a target job. The system used to conduct the oral interview will determine its degree of accuracy and thoroughness.

It is recommended that law enforcement agencies utilize a behavioral-based interview system, which includes the following criteria:

- Identifying the essential job, role, task skills, behavior, and traits desired to perform successfully in a target job.
- Reviewing the profile and/or background of the candidate to formulate personal history questions which specifically apply to job related tasks or essential job functions.
- Designing interview questions to evaluate the skills, behaviors, and traits desired for a target job.
- Training interviewers to gather and evaluate candidate data.
- Monitoring the process for continuous improvement.

Behavioral-based interviews function on the understanding that past performance is the best indicator of future performance. Once again it is on this one point that all psychologists, sociologists, recruiters, and personnel experts agree. The behavioral-based interview system will compare the candidate's past performance with the criteria identified for job success. This is the key to identifying candidates with the potential for job success.

The behavioral-based interview system should be used for all entry-level, promotional, and special assignments where an interview is required. The oral interview is a form of testing and must meet the requirement of validity. Validity requires that a testing instrument must measure job-related requirements only.

Identifying Candidate Criteria for Job Success

The law enforcement agency should identify the knowledge, skills, abilities, behaviors, and traits desired for the target job. This includes both the hard skills (technical ability) and soft skills (behaviors and traits) desired for a successful law enforcement officer. Remember the information from Chapter 1 on emotional intelligence in contrast to one's intelligence quotient.

If the law enforcement agency has a job-task analysis that has been completed for the target job within the last five years, it should be used as a resource to develop selection criteria. If a job-task analysis is not available or it was not done within the last five years, then the agency should attempt to complete one.

Employers obviously must know what the essential functions of a particular job are, if they are to make informed decisions about a person's ability to perform the job and defend those decisions in court should the need arise. However, defining the essential functions of a job is more art than science. The Americans with Disabilities Act offers little guidance. It merely states that consideration shall be given to the employer's judgment as to what functions of a job are essential, and if the employer has prepared a written job description for advertising or interviewing for the job, this description shall be considered evidence of the essential functions of the job. Regulations issued by the Equal Employment Opportunity Commission are more helpful. They state that essential functions include only fundamental, not marginal, job functions. The regulations set out several reasons for considering a job function essential: the position exists to perform that particular function; there are a limited number of employees to whom the function can be given; or the position is so specialized that employees were hired because of their expertise or ability to perform it.

The burden of defending the designation of a function as essential falls upon the employer (*Lenker v. Methodist Hospital* 210 F. 3d 792: 7th Cir. April 26, 2000). If a function is essential to the job, the Equal Employment Opportunity Commission recommends the following factors be considered: employee's judgment; written job description; the amount of time spent performing the function; the consequences of not performing the function; collective bargaining agreements; and the experience of job incumbents regarding the job.

The wise manager will take the time to identify the job-related requirements for a target job prior to conducting an oral interview.

Personal History Questions

Prior to conducting the oral interview, a review of the candidate's background investigation packet should be completed to develop any specific job-related questions. These questions should only be asked to clarify background information as it relates to job-related functions or essential job requirements. Otherwise, all candidates should be asked the same questions during the oral interview process. For example, a law enforcement officer candidate might be asked if his law enforcement certification is still valid. Maintaining this certification is an essential function of the job; therefore, this would be an appropriate question for an individual candidate.

Designing Behavioral-based Interview Questions

The interview questions asked should be based on obtaining information that measures a candidate's ability to perform job-related functions. These questions can be developed only after identifying the essential knowledge, skills, abilities, behaviors, and traits desired to perform successfully in a target job. Behavioral-based interview questions attempts to measure the degree to which a person has previously demonstrated the required or successful job-related traits. In behavioral-based interviewing, the questions measure an individual's past performance in relation to a dimension to predict future performance. In non-behavioral-based interviewing, the interviewer simply asks hypothetical questions that normally yield hypothetical answers. For example, if planning and organizing skills are an essential function of the job, a candidate may be asked about his planning and organizing skills.

The behavioral-based questions force the candidate to identify his or her past performance to a previously identified job related trait or behavior desired. Once again, hypothetical questions generally produce hypothetical answers indicating what a candidate might do in a given situation. Behavioral-based questions force the candidate to describe past behavior as it relates to job-related criteria. If the candidate has demonstrated the behavior in the past, especially the recent past, then there is a reasonable expectation that this is a learned behavior and may be expected in the future. If a trait or behavior has not been demonstrated in the past, then we can have no reasonable expectation that it will be demonstrated in the future, even if the candidate claims it will be. Questions that are not behavioral-based lead to selection errors, because the expectations of the candidate's performance and the actual performance do not match. The design of dimension-based interview questions requires prior training in this specialized area. A review of the chapter on legal issues provides information on what questions are and are not permissible to ask candidates. Selection criteria in Chapter 1 discusses the 12 areas that are identified as traits, behaviors, and abilities desirable for law enforcement officers. Interview questions should be designed to evaluate whether candidates have demonstrated these qualities currently or in the past.

Training Interviewers to Gather and Evaluate Candidate Data

It is recommended that before employers conduct behavioral-based interviews, that they be provided training on the interview process. It is the responsibility of the administration of a law enforcement agency to ensure that all interviewers receive sufficient training prior to evaluating candidates in a selection process. All interviewers should have thorough knowledge and understanding of the following areas: the target job being interviewed for; the purpose of the behavioral-based interview and its relationship to other components in the selection process; the job-related behaviors and traits identified as well as their relationship to job performance; the techniques of observing and recording behavior; how to use the rating form and consensus building; and the logistical preparations required to conduct the oral interview process. Most important is the training related to both the legal and human resource mandates regarding the interview of job candidates. Please remember that a job interview like all other components of the hiring process is a test; therefore, validity and reliability requirements apply. All interview questions must be job-related. Additionally, each candidate should be asked the same questions with the exception of those questions that are asked to clarify a response or to clarify information provided by the applicant. There are applicable laws that establish guidelines for what may and may not be asked of a job candidate. Both legal and human resource staff counsel should be utilized to critique and recommend interview questions for job candidates. In the appendix at the end of this chapter there is a list of questions that may not be asked by an employer.

It is recommended that at least three persons be utilized to conduct a behavioral-based interview session. It should be predetermined that one of the three individuals will ask all of the questions that have been selected for the target job. All three individuals on the interview panel will rate the candidate; however, one individual will have the additional responsibility for asking all questions and any additional questions strictly for clarification. It is critical that the person designated as the interviewer during the behavioral-based interview process obtain specific training on how to develop and ask dimension-based questions. This training should include the other areas as previously identified for the other members of the interview panel.

Another essential purpose of any oral interview is to evaluate the candidate's oral communication skills. A law enforcement officer must be able to demonstrate effective oral communication. This effective oral communication must occur during times of conflict and disorder. It is a pre-hire qualification. Therefore it is a skill that a candidate should bring to the job.

Monitoring the Interview Process for Continuous Improvement

Once a law enforcement agency has developed and implemented a behavioral-based interview process for any and all target jobs, this system must be "fine tuned" along the way. The roles, functions, and tasks of a job do not remain static. Therefore, as a target job is reevaluated to ensure that essential job functions and successful behaviors and traits are still valid, the behavioral-based interviews must also be modified. A law enforcement administrator should be assigned responsibility for designing, training, and implementing the behavioral-based interview process. Law enforcement managers should be involved in selecting candidates under their command. However, they should be trained and coached by an administrator who has developed these skills and has a thorough understanding of the behavioral-based interview system. The administrator and interviewers alike will discover that the questions initially developed might be effective in evaluating a candidate's ability to demonstrate job-related behaviors and traits. However, new questions may be developed that are more effective.

A critique of the behavioral-based interview process following a round of interviews to select successful job candidates will ensure that the law enforcement agency remains progressive in its approach to interviewing job candidates.

Appendix 12-1
Questions Employers Cannot Ask During a Job Interview

- Your age
- Date of birth
- Birthplace
- Ethnic background
- Religious beliefs
- Native language
- Marital status
- Date of marriage
- Whether your spouse is employed
- How much your spouse earns
- Whether you are pregnant
- Whether you have had an abortion
- The number of dependent children living with you
- To explain all gaps in your employment record (i.e., to ascertain if you have taken any time off to have children)
- Whether you have any physical or emotional defects before a conditional job offer is made (But an interviewer can ask whether you have any job-related defects.)

Recommendations and Key Points for Conducting Oral Interviews

1. Fundamentally there are two types of interview questions that are theoretical or behavioral-based interview questions.
2. It is recommended that the oral interviews be behavioral-based. This means interview questions are based on job-related knowledge, skills, abilities, behaviors, and traits.
3. Behavioral-based interviews function on the understanding that past performance is the best indicator of future performance.
4. The behavioral-based interview will compare the candidate's past performance with the criteria identified for job success and assist in determining if a candidate has the requisite skills and abilities necessary.
5. All interview questions must be job related and valid.
6. Training is required for the individual developing job-related and valid interview questions.
7. All persons evaluating the interviewee should be provided information on how to properly evaluate the candidate's responses in comparison to the job dimension criteria.
8. Behavioral-based interview questions should be modified or updated as dimensions for the job change.
9. Prior to conducting the behavioral-based interview, a review of the candidate's background investigation packet should be completed to develop any specific job-related questions. These questions are for the sole purpose of clarifying background information as it relates to the job-related criteria.
10. An essential purpose of any oral interview is to evaluate the candidate's oral communication skills.

Chapter 13

Personal History Questionnaire

The Purpose of the Personal History Questionnaire

The personal history questionnaire, sometimes called a confidential questionnaire, is a document that must be filled out completely and thoroughly by a law enforcement candidate in his or her own handwriting or typed. Prior to starting a background investigation, the investigator needs a personal history questionnaire completed by the candidate. For the background investigation to be thorough, the questionnaire must be complete, accurate, and provided to the background investigator in a timely manner. The candidate must formally attest to the truth of the information provided in the document and sign it indicating so. Failure to complete the personal history questionnaire should be considered to be a "disqualifier," and a result in the candidate's being dismissed from the selection process. An incomplete or inaccurate questionnaire should be a red flag for the investigator requiring a thorough examination at a minimum. The candidate should be given a specific date to return the completed personal history questionnaire to continue the application process.

The personal history questionnaire is the foundation for all investigative leads in the background investigation process. This document shall be referred to frequently by the background investigator. Should any information be obtained that is in conflict with the information provided on the personal history questionnaire, the investigator must determine why there is a discrepancy on the document. If the investigation reveals that the candidate either purposely omitted relevant information or was untruthful in his or her response, it is recommended that the candidate be rejected for employment. The background investigator should conduct an interview with the candidate prior to him or her completing the personal history questionnaire. During this interview, the background investigator should provide a thorough and complete explanation of how to complete this document, and the requirement that it be thorough and accurate, to be considered for hire. Prior to obtaining candidate information, a waiver should be signed by the candidate so that the investigator may legally access various privileged and confidential background information sources relative to the candidate. The personal history questionnaire, along with the law enforcement agency's background investigation procedures, provides an overview of how to complete the background investigation. The information requested on the personal history questionnaire should match the information being requested in the law enforcement agency's background investigation procedures packet.

Prior to questioning an applicant on the personal history questionnaire the investigator should familiarize themselves with the agency's legal and general orders requirements. At no time should questions be asked regarding an applicant's health, medical history, vision, hearing, and so forth. The Americans with Disabilities Act of 1990 makes it unlawful to inquire about an applicant's medical condition, or to conduct any medical tests, until after the applicant has been offered a "conditional offer of employment." While investigators cannot assure that such information will not be disclosed by an interviewee, the investigator should be careful not to solicit this information and restrict any follow-up on information inadvertently received. Additionally, Chapter 19 on legal considerations gives some information on what questions are and are not permissible to ask candidates.

Documents Included with the Personal History Questionnaire

The following documents must be obtained at a minimum from the applicant, and examined to verify compliance with the agency's requirements as part of the personal history questionnaire. All documents with the exception of the record of naturalization may be photocopied and the originals returned to the applicant. Federal law prohibits duplication of the Record of Naturalization. The pertinent information from this document may be recorded and attested to by the investigator.

1. Birth certificate
2. High School diploma or GED test
3. College transcripts
4. Marriage certificate
5. Dissolution of marriage papers (if applicable)

6. Military discharge or certificate of service (if applicable)
7. Driver's license
8. Naturalization papers (if applicable)

Recommendations and Key Points for Using a Personal History Questionnaire

The following recommendations are made concerning the personal history questionnaire:

1. The personal history questionnaire precedes the background investigation and matches the background investigation categories.
2. The personal history questionnaire is a primary source document to guide the background investigator concerning the applicant's personal history.
3. The personal history questionnaire should be filled out in the candidate's own handwriting or typed and provide all the information requested, accurately and in a timely manner.
4. The candidate attests to the truth of all the information provided on the personal history questionnaire and signs it.
5. Failure to complete the personal history questionnaire document should be considered a "disqualifier" and the candidate dismissed from the application process.
6. Prior to obtaining candidate information, a waiver should be signed by the candidate so that the investigator may legally access various privileged and confidential background information sources relative to the candidate.
7. If the investigation reveals that the candidate either purposely omitted relevant information or was untruthful in his or her response, it is recommended that the candidate be disqualified for employment.
8. At no time should questions be asked regarding an applicant's health, medical history, vision, hearing, and so forth. The Americans with Disabilities Act of 1990 makes it unlawful to inquire about an applicant's medical condition, or to conduct any medical tests, until after the applicant has been offered a "conditional offer of employment."

9. There are eight documents that must be obtained at a minimum from the applicant, and examined to verify compliance with the agency's requirements as part of the personal history questionnaire.

10. Federal law prohibits duplication of the Record of Naturalization. The pertinent information from this document may be recorded and attested to by the investigator.

Chapter 14

Conducting Background
Investigations

Introduction

The background investigation process is a vital part of the overall selection process for determining and selecting the best qualified person applying for a position within a law enforcement organization. In fact, every law enforcement agency must have a background investigation process. This is because high moral character is a pre-hire qualification for all law enforcement officers. It is important for the background investigation to be performed in a thorough and impartial manner. This is best accomplished through proper planning and by having an organized, prepared plan for each step of the process.

The purpose of a background investigation is to obtain information relating to the candidate's suitability (or non-suitability) for law enforcement employment relative to his or her behavioral history and character. This determination cannot easily be assessed through other segments of the selection process. In addition to possible past criminal behavior of the candidate, personality traits, skills, work habits, maturity level, and the ability to get along with people, the ability to respond appropriately to stressful situations is revealed and assessed during a thorough background investigation.

A thorough background investigation may be effectively used to screen candidates who otherwise seem suitable for law enforcement work. A study conducted several decades ago indicates the value of the background investigation process. Cohen and Chaiken, for example, in their study of New York law enforcement candidates, found that candidates who were rated as excellent by the background investigators had the lowest incidence of misconduct (36 percent had complaints filed), whereas the candidates termed poor had the highest incidence of misconduct, of which 68 percent had complaints filed (Cohen & Chaiken, 1973).

Law enforcement officers are granted a myriad of social powers, including, under certain circumstances, the taking of life and the deprivation of civil liberty. Law enforcement administrators have a tremendous responsibility to select only those officers with the character and ethics that are deserving of these powers. High moral character is the disposition to "do which reason determines is the best course of action based on ethical principles," rather than to allow personal feelings and desires to dictate which actions are taken. Consequently, candidates with high moral character are the ones who become the most professional and respected members of the department.

Background Investigator Guidelines

Background investigations are guided by two important and controlling factors: the need to obtain as much relevant information as possible on each candidate; and federal and statutory laws that prohibit eliciting certain information concerning the candidates. These laws include the Civil Rights Act of 1964, the Rehabilitation Act of 1973, the Civil Rights Act of 1991, and the Americans with Disabilities Act of 1990. These laws contain a number of specific provisions designed to assist in preventing discrimination in employment. Among the provisions are prohibitions for eliciting information from candidates prior to employment, which would indicate the candidate's race, color, religion, sex, national origin, disability, age, or ancestry.

The Civil Rights Act of 1991, Section 106 states, "It shall be unlawful employment practice for a respondent, in the connection with the selection of referral of applicants or candidates for employment or promotion, to adjust the scores of, use different cutoff scores for, or otherwise alter the results of, employment related tests on the basis of race, color, religion, sex, or national origin."

The Civil Rights Act of 1964, Section VII, requires that an agency cannot use a test standard that demonstrates adverse or disparate impact against a protected class (female, racial minority) unless the test standard is "job related." The Equal Employment Opportunity Commission has defined adverse impact as a protected class passing a test at a less than 80 percent rate of white males. A test with first impact can be used if there is data to show that the test standard is job related.

The background investigator must conduct the comprehensive investigation as a "fact-finding" process. Factual information about the candidate is the sole objective of the investigator, not evaluating or judging the information obtained. To do so could result in a subjective or biased background investigation, which would not only be inappropriate and possibly expose the agency to civil court action, but would also fail to serve the best interests of the department and respective candidate. There are many agencies that allow their investigators to comment on or evaluate the information obtained about the job applicant. However, it is not recommended because of the potential risk of the appearance of bias.

The evaluation of the information received, and therefore the decision to either accept or reject the candidate for further inclusion in the department's selection process, is made by those administrators responsible for such decisions. Those consequential decisions should be made relative to the department's vision, mission, goals, and values. The purpose of a selection process, simply put, is to find the "best" candidate fit for the department.

If a candidate's background information gives the agency reason to believe that the candidate either does not possess compatible values or may be resistant to the manner, direction, or speed in which the department is committed to its vision, mission, and goals, then rejection of the candidate must seriously be considered. The hiring rule recommended to all law enforcement agencies is that if there is a serious question as to the acceptance or rejection of a candidate, the final decision should be one that is in the best interest of the department, not of the candidate.

At the onset of the background process, a waiver (release) is required to be signed by the candidate, so that the investigator may legally access various privileged and confidential background information sources relative to the candidate. This release also enables current and former employers to legally provide the candidate's employee records to the investigator on request. However, employers are not legally compelled to provide this information.

The starting point for the background investigation is the personal history questionnaire. For the background investigation to be thorough, the questionnaire must be complete, accurate, and provided by the candidate to the background investigator in a timely manner. The candidate formally attests to the truth of the document and signs it. Failure to complete the form should be considered a "disqualifier" and grounds for dismissing the candidate from the process; an incomplete or inaccurate questionnaire should be a red flag requiring thorough examination at a minimum.

The personal questionnaire is the foundation for the background investigation process, and is referred to frequently by the investigator. Should information be obtained that is in conflict with the information provided on the personal history questionnaire, the investigator must determine why there is a discrepancy on the document. If the investigation reveals that the candidate either purposely omitted relevant information or was untruthful in his or her response, it is recommended that the candidate be rejected for employment.

Background Investigation Information Sources

Information sources that should be investigated include all those listed below, although not limited to this preliminary list.

- **Criminal history record:** Criminal history information includes criminal arrests or convictions, fines, sentences, confinement in jailor prison, probation history, and all pertinent dates and locations concerning the above, to include courts of record and case numbers.
- **Traffic record:** Information in this category includes traffic violation history, operator's license type, history and status to include points assessed, restrictions imposed, and any financial responsibility encumbrance relative to the candidate's auto insurance status.
- **Credit check:** Financial credit history and rating, which include outstanding loans and balances owed, history of any foreclosures, bankruptcies, late payments, and overall record of whether the candidate has fulfilled all outstanding financial obligations pursuant to the terms of the respective loans.

The credit history of all law enforcement applicants can provide significant insight to help identify the most qualified candidates. The credit history of a police applicant should receive an extensive review by the administrator. The credit history itself may reveal a history of critical behaviors demonstrated by the applicant that are job related.

The credit history may demonstrate the following key behaviors that are critical to a law enforcement officer's performance.

1. Use of credit is related to high moral character. The demonstrated ability to make repayments of bills as promised within a timely manner.
2. Responsibility. The applicant demonstrated the ability to live within his financial means of support.
3. Commitment. Candidates demonstrate their ability to keep their commitment to ultimately pay all creditors.
4. Decision-making and judgment. Candidate demonstrates an ability to use credit judiciously and not become over-extended financially on non-essential items.

A critical review of an applicant's credit history helps an organization identify the best candidates within the candidate pool while also confirming those unsuitable for the job. The credit history of an applicant should not be used as the sole criteria for dis-qualifying an applicant. It should be supported by other compatible job-related behaviors.

- **Past and current employers:** Included in this section are dates of employment, reasons for discharge or leaving employment, record of absenteeism or tardiness, ability to work with co-workers and others, any personnel disciplinary or exemplary actions, and overall performance evaluations. A key question to be asked is whether the previous employer would hire the candidate again if he or she chose to apply.
- **Personal references:** Current and past personal and professional references are usually investigated through in-person interviews. The objective of the interviews is to reveal experiences and incidents concerning the candidate that reflect his or her personal habits, character, and personality. It is very important to add "developed references" by finding out those persons who may have had issues with the candidate. Developed references often provide a much different perspective than interviews with the references listed on the application form.
- **Family interviews:** The law enforcement position can apply stress to the family ties of a candidate. The unusual shifts

being worked, the stress of handling conflict on a routine basis, and the perception of others about officers can create difficulties. The family of a candidate should be carefully interviewed and their support (or lack of support) indicated in the background investigation report.

- **Current and former addresses, neighbors:** The investigation should encompass a residential history of the candidate. In addition to listing all current and former addresses, as much information as possible about the candidate's interaction with neighbors should be obtained. Neighbors in the area of the candidate's home should be personally contacted, if possible. Neighbors can identify unusual, inappropriate, or exemplary behaviors by the candidate that might reflect on the character of the candidate; they are unlikely to freely speak with the investigator on the telephone.

- **High school and college records:** Academic records are reviewed to confirm the attainment of diplomas and degrees by the candidate, ensuring that the application is correct. Grade point averages (GPAs) are revealed, along with the major courses of study that indicate a candidate's experience and academic history. Involvement in extracurricular activities may also be reviewed if the candidate is a relatively recent graduate.

- **Military records:** Military records should be carefully verified. Dates of service, types of discharge, occupation within the military, transfers, and rank attained are included in this informational source.

- **Other law enforcement application records:** These records include all information developed by other agencies where the candidate has applied. Frequently, candidates apply for various law enforcement positions in the same time period. It is useful for one law enforcement agency to request all selection process information found in another agency, especially if the other agency includes a process or action not currently being taken by the investigator. Consistency in the results of comparable testing should be reviewed.

Often identifying the reason another agency rejected the candidate may show cause that the candidate is unsuitable for hiring. It is also helpful to know if the candidate is likely to be hired soon by the other agency. If so, committing additional time and expense may not be appropriate until the candidate has indicated an intention to accept the agency's potential offer for employment.

Summary

The background investigation is one of the most important parts of the selection process. Past behavior is the best predictor of future behavior, and can be a precursor of what can be expected once the candidate is hired. It is essential that the personal history questionnaire be thorough, and completed by the applicant for the background investigator to review. A comprehensive and complete investigation is required to ensure that the candidate has the necessary character and temperament to successfully fulfill the mission of the department. Accurate, thorough documentation is required to show the basis for any dismissal from the hiring process, and to show the agency's due diligence in hiring the best available candidates.

Recommendations and Key Points for a Background Investigation

The following recommendations are made concerning background investigations in the hiring process.

1. A background investigation is required for all law enforcement candidates, regardless of agency size or type.
2. A background investigation assists in helping to select the most qualified person or persons applying for a position within a law enforcement organization.
3. A good and thorough background investigation is established by prior planning and preparation.
4. The objective of a background investigation is to obtain information relative to the candidate's suitability or non-suitability for employment within the law enforcement agency, relative to his or her behavioral history and character.
5. The law enforcement administrators have a tremendous responsibility to select only those candidates with the characters and ethics that are deserving of the powers of law enforcement officers.

6. The candidates with character are the ones who become the most professional and respected members of a department.
7. Background investigators must conduct the background investigation consistent with all applicable state and local laws.
8. The background investigator must conduct a comprehensive investigation as a fact-finding process. Factual information of the candidate is the sole objective of the investigation, not evaluating or judging the information obtained.
9. Prior to conducting a background investigation, a waiver is required to be signed by candidates, which allows the investigator to access privileged and confidential background information from related sources.
10. The background investigation is preceded by the personal history questionnaire.
11. The background investigator uses the personal history questionnaire to provide complete and accurate information concerning the candidate.
12. If the investigation reveals that the candidate either purposely omitted relevant information or was untruthful in his or her response, it is recommended that the candidate be rejected for employment.
13. It is recommended that the background investigation review, at a minimum, ten separate and distinct areas of the candidate's background.
14. The credit history of all law enforcement applicants can provide significant insight to help identify the most qualified candidates. The credit history of an applicant should not be used as the sole criteria to disqualify an applicant. It should be supported by other compatible job-related behaviors.
15. Because past behavior is the best predictor of future behavior, the background investigation is a powerful tool used to make hiring decisions.

References

Cohen, B. and Chaiken, J. M. (1973). Police background characteristics and performance. The "Compleat" Officer. Lexington, Massachusetts. D.C. Heath and Company. p. 164.

Civil Rights Act of 1964

Rehabilitation Act of 1973

Civil Rights Act of 1991

Americans with Disabilities Act of 1990

Ohio Handicap Law

Chapter 15

Polygraph Examination

The polygraph or other suitable device an agency wishes to use to verify the integrity and truthfulness of a candidate's self-reporting information is a standard equation in the pre-employment process for most law enforcement agencies. The polygraph is useful in aiding an agency when determining whether a candidate has previous work-related or social problems that may eliminate that candidate from further consideration of a position with the law enforcement department. This phase works in tandem with the personal history questionnaire followed by verification from the background investigator. By focusing on areas of concern in the personal history questionnaire, a trained and experienced polygraphist can identify "untruths," false information, or general discrepancies from the candidate's statements on the personal history questionnaire.

This section shall provide useful guidelines in the administration of law enforcement employment polygraph examinations. It is not the intent of these guidelines to establish a standardized format, as there are many variables that apply to each individual process.

While conducting pre-employment polygraph examination, the polygraphist must abide by the most recent federal, state, and local laws. Additionally, each polygraphist must be sensitive to the needs, policies, and procedures of each law enforcement agency for which the examinations are conducted. Review of procedures by the local law director, solicitor, or designated legal authority is necessary.

Procedural Guidelines

The following guidelines are recommended in the administration of pre-employment polygraph examinations. These are suggestions and not meant to be requirements for any particular agency. Whether using a polygraph, the following guidelines should be considered.

Candidates making a request not to take a polygraph should be handled on a case-by-case basis. However, if required, it should apply to all candidates.

Pre-offer polygraph examinations are generally conducted prior to any conditional job offer. Pursuant to ADA, prior to a conditional job offer an employer must exercise care in not making any inquiries that could likely reveal a disability under this Act.

Post-offer examinations can be conducted at any time during the pre-employment process, as long as a conditional offer of employment has been made. It is suggested that the optimum time to conduct a post-offer examination is after the physical fitness test (if applicable), a background investigation, and a medical and psychological history of the candidate have been conducted. Any concerns or discrepancies that come to light during these processes can be verified through the polygraph examination.

Although polygraph examinations are used in both pre-conditional and post-conditional offer stages in law enforcement hiring, the Americans with Disabilities Act (ADA) limits the scope of the pre-offer medical inquiry.

Only an authorized member of the prospective employer should schedule a polygraph examination of candidates. All law enforcement agencies are encouraged to conduct pre-employment polygraph examinations on all prospective employees, both sworn and civilian. The need for integrity and confidentiality in a public safety agency necessitates taking this action to provide due diligence in the hiring process. This protects the agency and public employer from any potential negligent hiring issues later, should they develop.

Prior to administering any pre-employment polygraph examination, the polygraphist should review all available employment-related documents pertaining to the candidate. These documents can include, but not necessarily be limited to, the employment application, the background investigation, and the personal history report or self-report summary. The polygraphist needs a working knowledge of the information contained in the above items. Only by proper preparation can the polygraphist learn of possible areas that may require special attention.

As with other types of examinations, pre-employment polygraph examinations can be administered only to persons who voluntarily undertake the examination. A release/waiver form indicating such voluntary consent must be signed prior to the examination. Many agencies use the same release/waiver form that is used for specific issue criminal examinations. If an agency decides to utilize a polygraph as part of the selection process, it should be required for all candidates. If the candidate is medically unable to take the test at the time it is offered, he or she should be allowed to take the test at such time as he or she is medically capable.[1] While it should go without saying, it is important that the polygraphist verify the identity of the person being tested. This can be accomplished by viewing photographic identification, such as a driver's license, and comparing the signature to a document signed in the presence of the polygraphist, usually the release/waiver form.

It is recommended that the employer receive a detailed written report from the polygraphist upon completion of the examination. If a decision is made to remove a candidate from further consideration of employment, it must be based on job related and legally defensible, documented grounds. Therefore, the requirement of documentation from the polygraphist as to his or her findings is imperative.

The polygraph exam functions best as a screening-out tool for unsuitable candidates. It is used to uncover behaviors that are incompatible with the integrity required of police officers. Decision-support is the most obvious goal of a law enforcement employment polygraph screening process.

What Should Be Asked of Candidates?

At each stage of the hiring process, all candidates must be treated uniformly. Deviations can give rise to a discrimination suit by any candidate who has been rejected from further consideration of employment.

The following are some recommended areas of inquiry in the pre-offer stage:

- Driving record
- Criminal Activity
- Past employment job trouble
- Theft
- Employee theft
- Fraud

---

[1] Note: The candidate(s) would have to reapply if the hiring list expires before they are medically capable of taking the examination.

- Gambling addictions
- Un-American activity
- Credit history
- Falsifying the application
- Current illegal drug use, sales or possession

The following are recommended areas of inquiry in the post-offer stage:

- Illegal drug use/sales/possession
- Medical history
- Mental history
- Use of alcohol

It is important that the employer's legal department approve the areas of inquiry of both pre-offer and post-offer examinations.

Reporting Procedures

If an agency requires written reports, the polygraphist should ensure that each area of inquiry is addressed in the report. Admissions are to be as detailed as possible without becoming too wordy. When necessary, the report should suggest those areas requiring further inquiry and possible further polygraph testing. It should be stressed to the law enforcement agency, that any hiring decisions not be based solely on the results of the polygraph. One exception to this rule would be admissions that are made during the polygraph interview that would normally eliminate a candidate. The written report by the polygraphist should make no references to his or her personal opinion concerning the candidate. It is suggested that the polygraphist not provide any recommendations "to hire" or "not to hire" within the report. The polygraphist should remain objective in his or her report findings. This is the responsibility of the hiring agency and the results of the polygraph must be considered as merely one of many areas to be considered in hiring candidates.

Pursuant to ADA, portions of a post-offer polygraph examination may be considered confidential medical records. This would include, but not necessarily be limited to, medical history, psychological history, and usage of alcohol and/or drugs. As such, this information must be documented in a separate report and placed in a "confidential medical file" away from the candidate's regular personnel file. Some agencies forward these reports to the physician conducting the medical examination on the candidate. A sample of a disclaimer that may be used is stated below.

Example of Disclaimer:

> *In order to comply with the rules and regulations contained within the Americans with Disabilities Act, the information contained within this report is being documented on a separate form and is required by law to be filed in a separate and confidential medical file away from the prospective employee's regular personnel file.*

It is critical that the polygraphist follow all state laws and regulations regarding pre-employment inquiries and reports. For example, in Ohio, pre-employment polygraph examinations are considered public record. The polygraphist and the agency must always be cognizant of this fact when a report is made. The polygraphist must follow the retention schedule as established by the agency and purge report files as the schedule dictates.

Does the Polygraph Affect a Pregnancy?

A pregnant woman should not be tested on the polygraph. The polygraph instrument does not have any physical effect on the pregnant woman or the unborn child. However, the woman may claim that the stress of taking the polygraph had a negative physical affect on her child. It is suggested that the polygraphist have an agreement in writing with the agency that all candidates who are found to be pregnant will not be examined during the pregnancy. It is stressed that once the candidate is no longer pregnant and is considered medically capable; she will be placed in a position on the eligibility list to be considered next for employment. She should be given the opportunity to be administered a pre-employment polygraph examination ahead of all others at that particular time. This, in essence, would be providing the candidate with an alternative that the EEOC requires in situations such as this.

What if a Candidate Does Not Want to Take a Polygraph?

A polygraph examination should not be given to someone who does not want to take the examination or refuses to sign a release/

waiver form. Should the candidate refuse to take the polygraph examination, written procedures should indicate that the candidate would be excluded from the remainder of the hiring process. The candidate should be made clearly aware of this fact before being eliminated from the eligibility list. Unless the candidate should provide a physician's letter certifying legitimate health reasons for not taking a polygraph test, there should be no exceptions to this requirement. If a certifying physician's letter is provided, candidates in this situation should be handled on a case-by-case basis.

Procedures to Consider During the Polygraph Process

Prior to the actual testing, the polygraphist shall explain the polygraph procedure and prepare the candidate for the actual test.

Prior to the test, the polygraphist shall review each test question with the candidate. An examination will immediately cease on the request of the candidate. A refusal to answer any interview question should be considered as a refusal to take the examination and the testing procedure will be terminated. The candidate will be made aware that the refusal to take the examination or answer all questions will be grounds for elimination from the hiring process.

When conducting employment polygraph examinations, the polygraphist shall abide by the Code of Ethics and Standards and/or Principles of Practice of all associations to which the polygraphist holds current membership.

All candidates who are earmarked for the same academy class and for position should go through the same hiring process. To make changes during the course of the recruitment and selection process could give rise for an individual to file a claim of discrimination.

It is the law enforcement agency's responsibility to develop policies for dealing with criminal admissions made during the course of the employment polygraph process.

The law enforcement agency should have a policy in place regarding a candidate who arrives for an examination and has any condition that prevents the candidate from taking the examination as scheduled.

The law enforcement agency should have a policy place regarding a candidate who arrives late for a scheduled polygraph examination. There should be a policy that addresses the entire hiring process and the implications of a candidate who arrives late for any portion of the hiring process.

One significant benefit of a law enforcement pre-employment polygraph screening process is that it may deter less suitable candidates from applying for law enforcement positions. Consequently, those candidates who do apply may be more likely to meet the hiring standards if the polygraph deterrent were not in place.

Appendix 15-1
Court Cases That Affect Pre-employment
Polygraph Examinations

Woodland v. City of Houston (731 F. Supp. 1304)

This case involves two individuals, John Woodland, who applied for employment with the Houston Fire Department, and Chris Goss, who applied for employment with the Houston Airport Police. This suit was filed against the City of Houston alleging that the city's pre-employment polygraph examinations were arbitrary and unreasonably intrusive under both the United States and Texas constitutions. The jury found that the questions asked during the polygraph examination were unreasonably intrusive under separate definition of the federal and state constitutional standards. Because this was a "class action" suit, it also applied to those individuals who had applied for employment with the Fire, Police and Airport Police Departments of the City of Houston since March 1980, and who were rejected because of some information or conclusion derived from the polygraph process. This included the pre-test interview and the polygraphist's final opinion. As a result of this suit, a permanent injunction was issued wherein the City of Houston is enjoined, directly or indirectly, from asking questions during the pre-employment process that do not have an arguable and rational basis for discovering whether an applicant possesses actual qualifications reasonably related to the particular job.

This injunction prohibits questions that:

- Intrude into privacy or privacy concerns and affairs beyond matters reasonably related to actual requirements for the job the applicant seeks;

- Have not been narrowly, specifically, and directly tailored to the applicant's potential for capable performance of the job; and
- Inquire into matters about which an organization can otherwise acquire through reasonable alternative methods with information it is legally entitled.

Moon v. Cook County Police and Corrections Merit Board
(U.S. District Court — Northern District of Illinois, 78C1572)

This case involved an individual by the name of Harold Moon, who sued individually and on behalf of similarly situated black persons to enforce the provisions of Title VII of the Civil Rights Act of 1964.

The Merit Board was using and continued to use the results of polygraph examinations, which, according to Moon, had a disparate impact on black persons for the position of a Correctional Officer in the Cook County Correctional Institution. A consent decree resolved all the issues raised by Moon.

It is important to note that while the two aforementioned cases may create some restrictions relative to conducting pre-employment polygraph examinations, the cases only apply within their respective jurisdictions.

Buchanan v. City of San Antonio
85 F.3d 196 (5th Cir. 1996)

This case involved a sheriff's deputy who had injured his back, applied to join the San Antonio Police Department, and was turned down on numerous occasions. The person filed suit under the Americans with Disability Act claiming that he was entitled to judgment, as a matter of law, because the City had subjected him to a physical examination before making an offer of employment. The law enforcement department had made an offer of employment, but it was conditioned on successful completion of "the entire screening process, which included physical and psychological examinations, a polygraph examination, physical fitness tests, an assessment board, and an extensive background investigation." The Court agreed that, because the offer was not conditioned solely on the medical examination, there was a violation of ADA. The case was remanded to the district court to determine whether the job offer was not given because of the medical examination.

Hartman v. City of Petaluma
4NDLR 346 (D.C. Cal. 1994)

A candidate for a law enforcement officer's position had indicated that he had used only a small volume of drugs in the past, writing on his application that he used only a total of one-half to one ounce of marijuana during his entire life and only had used a "small amount of cocaine during his entire life." The application then "failed" the polygraph examination and subsequently admitted that he had used the drugs, plus or minus a hundred times each. The Court determined that he could not prevail on an ADA claim for two reasons: first, if he was telling the truth about the drug use being small: he was only a "casual user" and, therefore, not an addict and not protected under the ADA. The second reason was that because of his lack of candor about his past drug use, the applicant was not "otherwise qualified" within the Americans with Disabilities Act.

EEOC Determination re: Pregnancy

In December 1995, a pre-employment polygraph examination was conducted at the request of the King County Department of Youth Services. During the pretest interview portion of this examination, the polygraphist learned that the applicant was pregnant. The polygraphist explained to both the applicant and the employer that it was his policy not to test pregnant women due to his concerns about the health of the candidate, her baby, and his concerns for liability.[2] The employer apparently did not suggest, or even consider, alternative remedies to this situation and refused to process the applicant's application any further. The applicant subsequently filed a civil suit claiming discrimination with the EEOC. In November 1996, the polygraphist received a "Determination" from EEOC, which reports a "finding of reasonable cause to believe that discrimination did occur" not only for King County's

---

[2] The International Association of Chiefs of Police (IACP) has published a "model polygraph testing policy," which recommends that pregnant women not be tested.

lack of any alternative program, but also against the examiner for refusing to give the applicant the examination.

Agencies that use pre-offer polygraph testing should consult with their personnel experts and local counsel to ensure test coverage is in compliance with ADA rules.

Recommendations and Key Points for a Polygraph Examination

The following recommendations are made for use of the polygraph examination in law enforcement officer hiring:

1. The polygraph is useful in aiding a law enforcement agency in determining whether a candidate has previous work-related or social problems that can eliminate a candidate from further consideration.
2. The polygraph examination works in tandem with the pre-employment history questionnaire by focusing on areas of concern.
3. While conducting pre-employment polygraph examinations, the polygraphist must abide by the most recent federal, state, and local laws.
4. The Americans with Disabilities Act prohibits medical inquiries at the pre-offer stage.
5. Candidates making a request not to take a polygraph, examination should be handled on a case-by-case basis; however, if required for the job, it should apply to all candidates.
6. Pursuant to the Americans with Disabilities Act, prior to an actual job offer, the employer must exercise care in not making any inquiries that could likely reveal a disability.
7. Post-offer examinations can be conducted anytime during the pre-employment process, as long as the conditional offer of employment has been made.
8. Only an authorized member of the prospective employer should schedule a polygraph examination of the candidates.
9. Prior to administering any pre-employment polygraph examination, the polygraphist should review all available employment-related documents pertaining to the candidate.

10. As with other types of examinations, pre-employment polygraph examinations can only be administered to persons who voluntarily undertake the examinations.

11. If the candidate is medically unable to take the pre-employment examination at the time it is offered, they should be allowed to take it at such time as they are medically capable, as long as the selection process is still in progress.

12. The polygraphist should verify the identity of the person being tested.

13. If the decision is made to remove a candidate from further consideration for employment, it must be based on job related and legally defensible, documented grounds.

14. The written report of the polygraphist should make no mention of his or her personal opinion concerning the candidate. The polygraphist must remain objective in his or her report findings.

15. Pursuant to the Americans with Disabilities Act, selected portions of a post-offer polygraph examination may be considered confidential medical records.

16. In Ohio, pre-employment polygraph examinations are considered public record.

17. It is recommended that a pregnant woman should not be given a polygraph examination. The instrument does not have any physical effect on the pregnant woman or the child; however, the woman may claim that the stress of the polygraph had a negative physical effect on her child.

18. Should a candidate refuse to take the polygraph examination, written procedures should indicate that the candidate would be excluded from the remainder of the hiring process.

19. Although polygraph examinations are used in both pre-conditional and post-conditional offer stages in law enforcement hiring, the Americans with Disabilities Act (ADA) limits the scope of the pre-offer medical inquiry.

20. The polygraph exam functions best as a screening-out tool for unsuitable candidates. It is used to uncover behaviors that are incompatible with the integrity required of police officers. Decision-support is the most obvious goal of a law enforcement employment polygraph screening process.

21. One significant benefit of a law enforcement pre-employment polygraph screening process is that it may deter less

suitable candidates from applying for law enforcement positions. Consequently, those candidates who do apply may be more likely to meet the hiring standards if the polygraph deterrent were not in place.

References

The following documents can be obtained by calling EEOC at 1-800-669-4000 or by calling the Commission's Publications Distribution Center at 1-800-669-3362 or writing to EEOC's Office of Communications and Legislative Affairs, 1801 L Street, NW, Washington, D.C., 20507.

"EEOC Enforcement Guidance: Pre-Employment Disability-Related Inquiries and Medical Examinations Under the American with Disabilities Act of 1990." May 94, Ref. No. 915.002.

"EEOC Enforcement Guidance on Pre-Employment Disability-Related Inquiries and Medical Examinations Under the Americans with Disability Act." Oct. 95, Ref. No. 915.002 (Update).

"EEOC Enforcement Guidance on the Americans with Disabilities Act and Psychiatric Disabilities." May 97, Ref. No. 915.002 (Update).

"Questions and Answers: The Americans with Disabilities Act and Hiring Police Officers." March 97.

Chapter 16

The Entry-Level Assessment Center

It is recommended that a law enforcement agency utilize an entry-level assessment center to screen for the most qualified candidates for law enforcement officer. An assessment center is a standardized testing process that evaluates the ability to perform specific job-related skills and behaviors. The assessment center uses scenarios that stimulate the functions of the target job. Assessment center results provide information that predicts successful job performance. Trained assessors evaluate candidate performance and behavior that reflects strengths and weaknesses in job-related skills. The assessment center generates performance-based information to support the hiring decision.

It is a law enforcement best practice to use an entry-level assessment center to identify the most qualified candidates. The entry-level assessment center is ideally back-loaded in the selection process. In other words, after all candidates have been eliminated that are unsuitable for the police job, the entry-level assessment center identifies the most qualified remaining in the candidate pool. The entry-level assessment center identifies candidates with the highest degree of job-related behaviors and traits.

As previously indicated, a law enforcement agency should use a recent job analysis and other survey instruments to identify the most desirable knowledge, skills, abilities, behaviors, and traits for police officer candidate. This information should be used to develop an entry-level assessment center. The services of a consultant might be utilized to build an in-house entry-level assessment center that can be modified and utilized as needed on an ongoing basis.

The Assessment Center Defined

The assessment center method has been used in law enforcement for approximately 20 years. It has largely been used as a management tool to promote law enforcement candidates to management positions. Using the assessment center method as a tool for selecting entry level candidates is relatively new in the law enforcement

147

profession. However, it has tremendous potential to increase the quality of law enforcement officers selected. Among all of the jobs in law enforcement for which the assessment center may be utilized, it is the entry-level job that will benefit most from using this selection method. This is because knowledge, skills, abilities, behaviors, and traits are the most critical to assess when a person enters into an organization for employment. It is those individuals who have been selected at the entry-level positions who are predominantly identified as managers to lead the organization for many years in the future.

What Is a Law Enforcement Assessment Center and What Is It Designed To Do?

An assessment center is a standardized testing process that evaluates the ability of a candidate to perform specific job-related skills and behaviors. The assessment center uses exercises or scenarios that simulate the skills of the target job. The assessment center provides information that predicts successful job performance. The results identify individual and group training needs. The assessment center results may also be used to support career planning and personal development. Trained assessors evaluate candidate performance and behaviors that reflect strengths and weaknesses in job-related skills. The assessment center generates performance-based information to support a variety of personnel decisions.

The assessment center has five essential elements, which are:

1. Multiple assessment scenarios
2. Multiple trained assessors,
3. Valid simulation exercises,
4. Measurable performance and behavioral dimensions, and
5. Ratings based on compiled performance scores.

Why Assessment Centers Work

An assessment center's validity is based on six fundamental principles:

1. Organize the assessment process around targeted dimensions.

2. Use current behaviors to predict future behaviors.
3. Use simulations to elicit job-related behavior to be observed recorded and evaluated.
4. Use input from multiple simulations to ensure the coverage of all targeted dimensions.
5. Use trained assessors to observe and independently evaluate the assessee's behavior.
6. Integrate data during an organized discussion in which two or more assessors systematically compare the behavior insights, and then relate those findings to each target dimension to reach an overall decision.

Assessment centers improve the accuracy of selection and development decisions by effectively diagnosing participants' behavioral strengths and development needs. Because of the job relatedness of the simulation, participants more readily accept selection and promotion decisions as fair and accurate. Participants also gain a better understanding of job requirements.

Assessment centers create a learning environment for participants. By taking part in an assessment center, participants can better understand the direction in which the organization and profession are going and prepare for the "journey." When managers are trained to be assessors, their skills increase in many other managerial tasks, such as conducting coaching and feedback discussions, and handling performance appraisals. When an Entry-Level Assessment Center is used by an agency, management should have a clear understanding of essential job functions and successful job-related traits and abilities.

The major advantage of an assessment center as the centerpiece of a pro-social approach to police selection is the development of an ideal behavioral model against which actual activities of candidates can be assessed. Using candidate behaviors in well-chosen structured exercises increases the chances for maximum reliability and validity compared with paper-and-pencil tests. The latter assume stable, measurable personality traits expressed across all situations. Assessment centers, on the other hand, allow for the possibility of unlimited trait-situation interactions. The assessment center is also easily customized to reflect a particular department's most frequent and important on-the-job problem situations (Metchik, 1999).

A disadvantage of this approach is that assessment centers are time consuming and expensive to develop and use. Their implementation often includes all-day workshops with orientations for evaluators and participants. Candidates are then run through the exercises themselves, after which the raters meet. Alternatively, some have suggested video-based assessment or computerizing the traditional assessment center model as much as possible. The costs may still be prohibitive.

Assessment center exercises can measure stress tolerance, how effectively anxiety is handled, and the candidate understands of his or her own abilities, strengths, and weaknesses. The possible choice of exercises is virtually limitless. It should be guided, however, by the results of formal and informal job analyses as well as the policy priorities of the police and community members of your specific jurisdiction (Metchik, 1999).

Reference

Metchik, E. (1999). An Analysis of the "Screening Out" Model of Police Officer Selection. *Police Quarterly*, 2(1), 79–95.

The Entry-Level Assessment Center

The real potential for growth in use of the assessment center method in law enforcement's current environment lies in our search for the contemporary law enforcement officer. He or she is customer-service oriented, is a team player, has high moral and ethical standards, has good written and oral communication skills, appreciates human diversity, has a positive attitude, and is a problem solver possessing good decision-making skills. The Entry-Level Assessment Center can evaluate these skills, knowledge, abilities, behaviors, and traits and more. There is a major difference between an Entry-Level Assessment Center and a promotional assessment center. In the entry level assessment, all job knowledge is removed from the simulations. Candidates are evaluated purely on their ability to demonstrate job-related abilities and traits in simulations not requiring prior law enforcement knowledge.

Most law enforcement agencies have a multi-step hiring process that usually comprises six to twelve steps. However, the main focus of this multi-step process is to screen for deficiencies that might result in job failure, rather than screening for strengths that will lead to job success. Such a process is largely effective in doing what it is designed to do, which is to screen for severe and obvious behavior deficiencies. When the Entry-Level Assessment Center is added to this process, the hiring agency seeks candidates possessing successful behavioral dimensions. In this era of community-based policing, we should be seeking candidates whose strengths are compatible with this philosophy. I suggest that agencies consider using an Entry-Level Assessment Center. You may discover that candidates appear desirable as potential employees until they are measured in an Entry-Level Assessment Center. The assessment center will identify candidates who are compatible with the agency's philosophies and expose candidates who are not. It may also identify the rank order in which candidates should be hired, based on results.

Ultimately, the Entry-Level Assessment Center will place candidates in one of three categories. The first of these categories is, the candidate is "very ready" for law enforcement service. The second is, the candidate is "currently ready" for law enforcement service. The third category is, the candidate is currently "not ready" for law enforcement service. The candidates will be given a raw and percentage score in each of the simulations and an overall score. The "very ready" candidates should have the highest priority in the hiring sequence, followed by the "ready" candidates. Candidates identified as "not ready" at this time should not be hired for at least one year, and must score in the "ready" category in a subsequent assessment center evaluation to be hired at a later time.

The Entry-Level Assessment Center should be used in conjunction with other components of the selection process and compliments the other methods (i.e., background investigation, written exam, medical examination, etc.). It should not be used as the sole criteria for selecting law enforcement officers.

Recommendations and Key Points for the Entry-Level Assessment Center

The following recommendations are made concerning the Entry-Level Assessment Center:

1. The assessment center method as a tool for selecting entry-level candidates is relatively new in the law enforcement profession.

2. It is the entry-level job that will benefit the most from using an assessment center. This is because the knowledge, skills, abilities, behaviors, and traits are most critical to assess when a person enters into an organization for employment.

3. An assessment center is a standardized testing process that evaluates the ability of the candidate to demonstrate specific job-related skills and behaviors.

4. The assessment center provides information that predicts successful job performance.

5. A true assessment center must have five essential elements.

6. An assessment center's validity is based on six fundamental principles.

7. Assessment centers improve the accuracy of selection and development processes by effectively diagnosing behavioral strength and development needs.

8. Due to the job relatedness of the simulation, participants more readily accept selection decisions as fair and accurate.

9. By taking part in an assessment center, candidates can better understand the direction the organization and profession is going and prepare for the journey.

10. There is a major difference between an Entry-Level Assessment Center and a promotional assessment center. In the entry level assessment, all job knowledge is removed from the simulations. Candidates are evaluated solely on their ability to demonstrate job related abilities and traits in simulations not requiring prior law enforcement knowledge.

11. You may discover that candidates appear desirable as potential employees until they are measured in an Entry-Level Assessment Center. The assessment center will identify candidates who are compatible with the agency's philosophies, and expose those candidates who are not.

12. After completing the Entry-Level Assessment Center, candidates will be scored as "very ready," "currently ready" or "not ready" at this time for law enforcement service.

13. The Entry-Level Assessment Center may identify the rank order in which candidates may be hired based on results.

14. The Entry-Level Assessment Center method should be used in conjunction with the other components to the selection process for hiring law enforcement officers.

Introduction

J. Nick Marzella, Ph.D., asks this question: "To Test or Not To Test, That Is the Question." With over 50 percent of all law enforcement agencies having some sort of psychological testing process, it is clear that agency administrators recognize a need to reduce the potential liability incurred by the selection of a person who may be emotionally unstable or be a high risk to an agency. Dr. Marzella also indicates that, unlike the assessment center, the psychological testing process is one that "selects out" a candidate that may incur risk, as opposed to "selecting in" a candidate that has positive characteristics (Marzella, 2000). Although psychological testing of candidates for employment to eliminate unsuitable individuals can be traced back to post World War II in the United States, the law enforcement profession did not generally begin to use psychological screening methods until the late 1960s, following urban riots in several cities. The 1968 National Advisory Commission on Civil Disorder called for screening methods that would improve the quality of law enforcement officers hired by eliminating high-risk candidates. The emphasis placed on personality traits in the 1960s became more focused on behavior in the 1970s and 1980s.

Why Use a Psychological Testing Process?

The most obvious reason for using a psychological testing process is liability. Damage awards against law enforcement agencies that have failed to screen out unstable officers have been granted to individuals.

Litigation is not the only reason to employ valid psychological screening processes. Communities can ill afford to hire officers with questionable character flaws. The very image of the agency is dependent on a consistent, appropriate application of the law. A single incident of dishonesty, abuse, discrimination, or violence by an officer can create the public perception of a lack of integrity within an agency. Community disrespect can result in a lack of cooperation that is so essential to a successful law enforcement agency. The power of arrest (taking away a person's freedom) and the power to use necessary force (up to and including deadly force that can take a person's life) are awesome responsibilities placed on individual officers. If a person is hired as an officer at risk for emotional instability, it can have tragic results.

Entry-Level Psychological Screening

Once an individual candidate meets the minimum requirements for a law enforcement position, a more difficult process begins to determine if the individual is suited for a law enforcement career. Very little is known about a law enforcement candidate until well after the selection process has begun.

At its best, the screening process can help to identify high-risk candidates before significant resources have been expended for training, equipment, and supervision in a probationary period. The earlier in the selection process that an unsuitable candidate is identified and eliminated, the more efficiently the agency can use its resources to deliver service to the community.

Psychologists cannot foresee the future potential of a candidate. However, the administration of a sound psychological testing process and clinical interview can indeed improve the selection of appropriate candidates. In spite of the obvious benefits that may be derived from psychological screening, controversy still exists regarding its use. Questions of adverse impact, reliability, personal intrusion, and consistency among evaluators are among the most salient issues that must be addressed.

The goal of psychological screening is to eliminate high-risk candidates while withstanding legal challenges and complying with civil mandates. The development of stringent guidelines need to be established to ensure that the specific testing process is sufficient. Care should be taken to ensure that the legal aspects of the particular process used have been reviewed by legal counsel.

Psychological Testing Considerations

The American Psychological Association (APA) has published guidelines for those involved in the psychological screening of law enforcement officers. APA's recommendations are based largely on research compiled by Dr. Robin Inwald, Jr. Dr. Inwald suggests some important considerations for designing a reasonable, defensible psychological screening process that are detailed below:

- Psychological testing should be used as one component of the overall selection process. Psychological recommendations should not be used as the sole criteria for a "hire/no hire" decision.
- Both formal and informal efforts should be made to clarify agency goals and psychological testing procedures for administrators.
- A rating system for evaluation should be developed that provides for more than a "yes" or "no" determination of psychological stability.
- Psychologists conducting the assessments should be familiar with not only the field of psychological testing for law enforcement officers, but should also be knowledgeable about law enforcement officers and their job functions.
- Written psychological tests should be validated for use with law enforcement candidates and the selected tests should avoid adverse impact based on sex and race.
- A clinical diagnosis or psychological "labeling" should be avoided, and a clinical assessment of overall emotional adjustment affecting specific job performance should be made.
- Written "job related" psychological reports should be prepared for each candidate tested, avoiding psychological jargon and "hospital" language.
- Psychologists should retain a "consultant's status" rather than performing selection tasks more appropriate for personnel officers.
- Only licensed psychologists adequately trained and experienced in psychological test interpretation and psychological assessment techniques should be retained to conduct psychological screening for law enforcement agencies.
- If a decision based even in part on psychological results is challenged, providers of the psychological testing services should be prepared to defend their procedures, conclusions, and all recommendations (Inwald, 1986).

The International Association of Chiefs of Police has established guidelines for psychologists providing services to law enforcement agencies. These guidelines are provided here for law enforcement agencies to ensure that psychological services provided meet these established benchmarks. It should be noted that these guidelines include conducting fitness-for-duty evaluations that are law enforcement officer retention issues.

Guidelines for Police Psychological Service
By the IACP Police Psychological Services Section

The IACP Police Psychological Service Section provides guidelines for professional psychological practice to the law enforcement community. The guidelines cover pre-employment psychological evaluations, psychological fitness-for-duty evaluations, officer-involved shootings, and peer support.

The guidelines reflect currently accepted minimum standards but will be periodically revised to reflect new developments in case law, psychometrics, professional practices, and research.

The IACP Board of Officers approved the following guidelines in 2005.

Pre-employment Psychological Evaluation Services Guidelines

Overview

The following statements are guidelines for professional practice in the area of pre-employment psychological evaluations of candidates for public safety positions. These positions include but are not limited to positions where incumbents have arrest authority or the legal authority to detain and confine individuals. These guidelines are presented as a recommended professional policy for public safety agencies and individuals who are charged with the responsibility of conducting defensible pre-employment psychological screening programs.

Psychologists must adhere to ethical principles and standards for practice, including the standards of the American Psychological Association.

Development

1. Pre-employment psychological assessments should be used as one component of the overall selection process.
2. Before conducting their own clinical assessments of candidates, practitioners should be familiar with the research literature available on psychological testing for public safety positions, as well as the state and federal laws relevant to this area of practice, including the Americans with Disabilities Act (ADA).
3. Except as allowed or permitted by law, only licensed or certified psychologists trained and experienced in psychological test interpretation and law enforcement psychological assessment techniques should conduct psychological screening for public safety agencies.
4. Data on attributes considered most important for effective performance in a particular position should be obtained from job analysis, interview, surveys, or other appropriate sources.
5. Efforts should be made to provide agency administrators with information regarding the benefits and limitations of psychological assessment procedures so that realistic goals may be set.
6. Provisions should be made for the security of all testing materials (e.g., test booklets). Provisions should also be made for the security of, access to, and retention of the psychological report and raw data.
7. Prior to the administration of any psychological instruments and psychologist interview, the candidate should sign an informed consent to the conditions of the evaluation. The informed consent should clearly state the agency is the client.

Testing

8. A test battery including objective, job-related, validated psychological instruments should be administered to the applicant. It is preferable that test results be available to the evaluator before screening interviews are conducted.
9. Written tests selected should be validated for use with public safety candidates.

10. If mail-order, Internet-based, or computerized tests are employed, the licensed or certified psychologist conducting the follow-up interview should verify and interpret individual results.

11. The pre-employment psychological evaluation must be conducted in accordance with the Americans with Disabilities Act (ADA). A psychological evaluation is considered "medical" if it provides evidence that could lead to identifying a mental or emotional disorder or impairment as listed in the DSM-IV, and therefore must only be conducted after the applicant has been tendered a conditional offer of employment.

Personality tests and other methods of inquiry that are not medical by the above definition and that do not include specific prohibited topics or inquiries may be conducted at the pre-offer stage. However, these assessments alone are not capable of determining a candidate's emotional stability and therefore would not constitute an adequate pre-employment psychological evaluation.

Interview

12. Individual, face-to-face interviews with candidates should be conducted before a final psychological report is submitted.

13. A semi-structured, job-related interview format should be employed with all candidates.

14. Interviews should be scheduled to allow for sufficient time to cover appropriate background and test results verification.

Evaluation

15. Public safety agency administrators directly involved in making employment decisions should be provided with written reports. These reports should evaluate the suitability of the candidate for the position based on an analysis of all psychological material including test data and interview results. Reports to the agency should contain a rating and/or recommendation for employment based on the results of the screening, justification for the recommendation and/or

rating, and any reservations that the psychologist might
have regarding the validity or reliability of the results.

16. While a clinical assessment of overall psychological suitability and stability may be made, clinical diagnoses or
psychiatric labeling of candidates should be avoided when
the goal of the assessment is to identify candidates whose
psychological traits may adversely affect specific job performance. In all cases, the screening should be focused on an
individual candidate's ability to perform the essential
functions of the position under consideration.

17. Specific cut-off scores should be avoided, unless there is
clear statistical evidence that such scores are valid and have
been cross-validated in research studies by the test developer
or in the agency where they will be used. If cut-off scores are
used, the report should acknowledge their use and the basis
for using the specific cut-off level. Conclusions concerning a
candidate's qualifications should be based on consistencies
across data sources rather than on a single source.

18. Clear disclaimers should be made so that reports evaluating
current emotional and behavioral traits or suitability for a
public safety position will not be deemed valid after a
specific period of time.

Follow-up

19. Care should be taken when using pre-employment test
results for purposes other than making pre-employment
decisions and for monitoring the candidate during the
probationary period. Follow-up research may be conducted
with agency approval and where individual identities are
protected. Pre-employment reports should not be used for
positions not expressly considered by the psychologist at the
time of the evaluation.

20. Continuing collaborative efforts by the hiring agency and
evaluating psychologist should be made to validate final
suitability ratings using behavioral criteria measures.

21. Each agency should maintain adverse impact analyses to
detect any discriminatory patterns of the psychological
screening program.

22. Psychologists should be prepared to defend their procedures, conclusions, and commendations if a decision based, even in part, on psychological results is challenged.

(Ratified by the IACP Police Psychological Services Section, Los Angeles, California, 2004.)

Psychological Fitness-for-Duty Evaluation Guidelines

The focus of this book is on hiring an entry level officer. However, I thought it would also be beneficial to provide information on conducting fitness for duty evaluations since this could be applicable for recruits in the academy or in the field prior to them completing their probationary period.

Purpose

The IACP Psychological Services Section developed these guidelines for use by public safety agencies and mental health examiners. These guidelines are not intended to establish a rigid standard of practice for psychological fitness-for-duty evaluations (FFDEs). Instead, they are intended to reflect the commonly accepted practices of the section members and the agencies they serve. Each of the guidelines may not apply in a specific case or in all situations. The decision as to what is or is not done in a particular instance is ultimately the responsibility of each agency and professional examiner.

Definition

A psychological FFDE is a formal, specialized examination of an incumbent employee that results from (1) objective evidence that the employee may be unable to safely or effectively perform a defined job and (2) a reasonable basis for believing that the cause may be attributable to psychological factors. The central purpose of an FFDE is to determine whether the employee is able to safely and effectively perform his or her essential job functions.

Threshold Considerations

1. Referring an employee for an FFDE is indicated whenever there is an objective and reasonable basis for believing that

the employee may be unable to safely or effectively perform his or her duties due to psychological factors. An objective basis is one that is not merely speculative but derives from direct observation, credible third-party report, or other reliable evidence.

2. FFDEs necessarily intrude on the personal privacy of the examinee and therefore should be conducted after the employer has determined that other options are inappropriate or inadequate in light of the facts of a particular case. The FFDE is not to be used as a substitute for disciplinary action.

3. If an employer is uncertain whether its observations and concerns warrant an FFDE, it may be useful to discuss them with the employer's examiner or legal counsel prior to mandating the examination.

Examiner Qualifications

4. In light of the nature of these evaluations and the potential consequences to the agency, the examinee, and the public, it is important for examiners to perform FFDEs with maximum attention to the relevant legal, ethical, and practice standards, with particular concern for statutory and case law applicable to the employing agency's jurisdiction. Consequently, these evaluations should be conducted only by a qualified mental health professional. At a minimum, the examiner should

   a. be a licensed psychologist or psychiatrist with education, training, and experience in the diagnostic evaluation of mental and emotional disorders;

   b. possess training and experience in the evaluation of law enforcement personnel; be familiar with the police psychology literature and the essential job functions of the employee being evaluated;

   c. be familiar with relevant state and federal statutes and case law, as well as other legal requirements related to employment and personnel practices (e.g., disability, privacy, third-party liability); and

   d. satisfy any other minimum requirements imposed by local jurisdiction or law.

5. When an FFDE is known to be in the context of litigation, arbitration, or another adjudicative process, the examiner should have particular training and experience in forensic psychological or psychiatric assessment. In such cases, the examiner should be prepared by training and experience to qualify as an expert in any related adjudicative proceeding.

Identifying the Client

6. The client in an FFDE is the employer, not the employee being evaluated, and this fact should be communicated to all involved parties at the outset of the evaluation. Nevertheless, the examiner owes an ethical duty to both parties to be fair and impartial and to honor their respective legal rights and interests. Other legal duties also may be owed to the examinee as a result of statutory or case law unique to the employer's or the examiner's jurisdiction.

7. Examiners should decline to accept an FFDE referral when personal, professional, legal, financial, or other interests or relationships could reasonably be expected to (a) impair their objectivity, competence, or effectiveness in performing their functions or (b) expose the person or agency with whom the professional relationship exists to harm or exploitation (e.g., conducting an FFDE on an employee who had previously been a confidential counseling or therapy client, evaluating an employee with whom there has been a business or significant social relationship). Similarly, an FFDE examiner should be mindful of potential conflicts of interest related to recommendations or the provision of services following the evaluation (e.g., referring an examinee to oneself for subsequent treatment). If such conflicts are unavoidable or deemed to be of minimal impact, the examiner should nevertheless disclose the potential conflict to all affected parties.

Referral Process

8. It is desirable that employers have FFDE policies and procedures that define such matters as circumstances that would give rise to an FFDE referral, mechanisms of referral

and examiner selection, any applicable report restrictions, sharing results with the examinee, and other related matters.

9. The employer's referral to the examiner should include, at a minimum, a description of the objective evidence giving rise to concerns about the employee's fitness for duty and any particular questions that the employer needs the examiner to address. In most circumstances, this referral should be documented in writing.

10. In the course of conducting the FFDE, it is usually necessary for the examiner to receive background and collateral information regarding the employee's past and recent performance, conduct, and functioning. The information might include, but is not limited to, performance evaluations, previous remediation efforts, commendations, testimonials, internal affairs investigations, formal citizen or public complaints, use-of-force incidents, reports related to officer-involved shootings, civil claims, disciplinary actions, incident reports of any triggering events, medical records, or other supporting or relevant documentation related to the employee's psychological fitness for duty. In some cases, examiners may ask the examinee to provide medical/psychological treatment records and other data for the examiner to consider.

11. When some portion of the information requested by an examiner is unavailable or is withheld, the examiner must judge the extent to which the absence of such information may limit the reliability or validity of his or her findings and conclusions before deciding to proceed. If the examiner proceeds with the examination, the subsequent report should include a discussion of any such limitations judged to exist.

Informed Consent and Authorization

12. An FFDE requires the informed consent of the examinee to participate in the examination. At a minimum, informed consent should include a description of the nature and scope of the evaluation; the limits of confidentiality, including any information that may be disclosed to the employer without the examinee's authorization; the potential outcomes and

probable uses of the examination; and other provisions consistent with legal and ethical standards for mental health evaluations conducted at the request of third parties.

13. In addition to obtaining informed consent, the examiner should obtain written authorization from the employee to release the examiner's findings and opinions to the employer. If such authorization is denied, or if it is withdrawn once the examination commences, the examiner should be aware of any legal restrictions in the information that may be disclosed to the employer without valid authorization. With valid written authorization, an examiner is free to disclose unrestricted information to the employer.

Evaluation Process

14. Depending on the referral question and the examiner's clinical judgment, an FFDE typically relies on multiple methods and data sources in order to optimize the reliability and validity of findings. The range of methods and data sources frequently includes

    a. a review of the requested background information (e.g., personnel records, medical records, incident reports or memos);

    b. psychological testing using assessment instruments (e.g., personality, psychopathology, cognitive, specialized) appropriate to the referral question(s);

    c. a comprehensive, face-to-face clinical interview;

    d. collateral interviews with relevant third parties if deemed necessary by the examiner; and

    e. referral to, and consultation with, a specialist if deemed necessary by the examiner.

15. Prior to conducting collateral interviews of third parties, care should be taken to obtain informed consent from the employer, the examinee, or from the third party, as appropriate. This should include, at a minimum, explanation of the purpose of the interview, how the information will be used, and any limits to confidentiality.

Report and Recommendations

16. Customarily, the examiner will provide a written report to the client agency that contains a description of the rationale for the FFDE, the methods employed, and whenever possible, a clearly articulated opinion that the examinee is presently fit or unfit for unrestricted duty. The content of the report should be guided by consideration of the terms of informed consent, the employee's authorization, the pertinence of the content to the examinee's psychological fitness, the employing agency's written policies and procedures, the applicable terms of any labor agreement, and relevant law.

17. When an examinee is found unfit for unrestricted duty, the report should contain, whenever possible, the following minimum information unless prohibited by law, agency policy, labor agreement, the terms of the employee's disclosure authorization, or other considerations:

    a. a description of the employee's functional impairments or job relevant limitations; and

    b. an estimate of the likelihood of, and time frame for, a return to unrestricted duty, and the basis for that estimate.

18. It is recognized that some examiners may be asked to provide opinions regarding necessary work restrictions, accommodations, interventions, or causation. Nevertheless, the determination as to whether or not a recommended restriction or accommodation is reasonable for the specific case and agency is a determination to be made by the employer, not the examiner.

19. The examiner's findings and opinions are based on all data available at the time of the examination. If additional relevant information is obtained after completion of the FFDE or if it is determined that the original evaluation was based on inaccurate information, the employer may request that the examiner reconsider his or her conclusions in light of the additional information. Reconsideration or re-evaluation also may be indicated in circumstances where an employee, previously deemed unfit for duty, subsequently provides information suggesting his or her fitness has been restored.

20. Decisions concerning whether and how the findings and opinions resulting from the FFDE are to be communicated to the examinee should be disclosed to all parties in advance of the examination whenever possible. Such decisions should be governed by standards of professional ethics, clinical considerations, statutory and case law, and any prior agreements with the employer and examinee.

21. Some agencies may find differences of opinion between or among the examiner and other health care professionals. Employers should be prepared to address these differences if they arise. In such cases, the employer may find it helpful to consider (a) any differences in the professionals' areas of expertise and knowledge of the employee's job and work environment, (b) the objective bases for each opinion, and (c) whether the opinion is contradicted by information known to or observed by the employer.

22. Agencies should handle FFDE reports in conformance with legal standards governing an employer's treatment of employee medical records.

(Ratified by the IACP Police Psychological Services Section, Los Angeles, California, 2004.)

Officer-Involved Shooting Guidelines

These guidelines were developed to provide information and recommendations on constructively supporting officers involved in a shooting. The field experience of members of the IACP's Psychological Services Section suggests that following these guidelines can reduce the probability of long-lasting psychological and emotional problems resulting from a shooting incident. These guidelines are not meant to be a rigid protocol and work best when applied in a case-by-case manner appropriate to each unique situation.

Agency Protocol Recommendations

1. Prior to any shooting incident, agencies are encouraged to train all officers, supervisors, and family members in acute stress and traumatic reactions and what to expect personally, departmentally, and legally after a shooting incident.

2. Prior to any shooting incident, it is in the agency's best interest to establish a working relationship with a trained,

licensed mental health professional who is experienced in the law enforcement culture as well as in providing post-shooting interventions. The department should notify the mental health professional as soon as possible and facilitate a post-shooting intervention by the mental health professional. Some guidelines for the mental health professional's intervention are addressed below.

3. Immediately after an incident, provide physical first aid and communicate emotional support and reassurance to involved officers and other personnel.

4. Offer the officer an opportunity to step away from the scene and away from media attention (by waiting at a remote location, for instance). When possible, place the officer with supportive peers or supervisors and return the officer to the scene only if strictly necessary. Personnel on the scene should help the officer follow departmental policies regarding talking about the incident before the initial investigation interviews. If the officer has an immediate need to talk about the incident, he or she should be provided with a resource that offers the officer confidentiality or privileged communication.

5. Ideally, the officer should be provided with some recovery time before detailed interviewing begins. This can range from a few hours to overnight. Officers who have been afforded this opportunity are likely to provide a more coherent and accurate statements. Providing a secure setting, insulated from the press and curious officers, is desirable during the interview process.

6. Explain to the officer what is likely to happen administratively during the next few hours and the reasons behind the planned actions. Within two days, explain the entire process of the investigation as well as any potential actions by the media, grand jury, or review board. Also, discuss any concerns raised by the officer. A summary of procedures can be provided in a written format that the officer can refer to during the first few hours after the incident.

7. It may be helpful to provide an information sheet or booklet that reviews the body's response to shooting incidents and what the officer can do to facilitate recovery. The officer can

refer to this information after the post-shooting intervention, and perhaps share it with significant others.

8. If the officer's firearm has been taken as evidence, it should be replaced as soon as possible. When this is not possible, the officer should be told why and when the weapon is likely to be returned. Officers, especially those in uniform, may feel vulnerable when unarmed and become concerned that an administrative action has been undertaken. It is desirable to assign an armed companion officer to stay with the officer under these circumstances.

9. If the officer has not been injured, the officer or a department representative should contact the family to inform them of the occurrence before other sources are able to do so. If the officer is injured, a department member, preferably one known to the family, should meet family members and drive them to the hospital. An offer to call friends, chaplains, and so on should be made to ensure that the family has an adequate support system available to them.

10. It may be desirable to provide the officer with a few days of administrative leave to protect him or her from possible retaliation by the suspect and to allow the officer to marshal his or her natural coping skills to deal with the emotional impact of the incident. Make sure that the officer understands that this is an administrative leave, not a suspension with pay.

11. It may be in the best interest of the officer and the agency to modify the officer's duties until the initial criminal investigation, internal shooting review board investigation, grand jury investigation, coroner's inquest, and district attorney's statements have all been completed. This practice protects the officer from potential legal and emotional problems that might arise from involvement in another critical incident before the first one has been resolved or from coming into contact with suspects or witnesses to the shooting while on the job.

12. Agencies, in cooperation with the affected officer, should consider the readiness of an officer to return to regular duties. For example, it may be preferable to work a different shift or a different beat for a period of time. It may also be

helpful to permit an officer to team up with a co-worker for several shifts.

13. If the officer has a published home telephone number, it may be advisable to have a friend or telephone answering machine screen telephone calls to prevent any annoying or threatening calls from reaching the officer or family members.

14. Whenever possible, an administrator should inform the rest of the department, or at least the officer's supervisors and his or her team, about the shooting. This practice will reduce the number of questions asked of those involved and will also help to deal with any rumors that may have arisen as a consequence of the event.

15. Agencies should make every effort to expedite the completion of administrative and criminal investigations and advise the officer of the outcomes as soon as possible. Lengthy investigations can cause distress to the officer.

16. Departments should assess the reactions of any other involved emergency service personnel (including dispatchers) and provide appropriate interventions as described above.

17. The option of talking to peers who have had a similar experience can be quite helpful to personnel at the scene. Peer support personnel may also be an asset participating in group interventions in conjunction with a mental health professional, and can be an asset in providing follow-up support. Family members may also greatly benefit from the peer support of family members or other officers who have been involved in shooting incidents. The formation and administrative backing of peer support and outreach teams for officers and family members may prove to be a wise investment after a shooting incident. However, peer support should never take the place of an intervention by a mental health professional.

18. Personal concern and support for the officer involved in the shooting, communicated from high-ranking administrators, can provide an extra measure of reassurance and comfort. The administrator does not have to comment on the situation, or make further statements regarding legal or

departmental resolution, but can show concern and empathy for the officer during this stressful experience.

19. Shootings are complex events often involving officers; command staff; union representatives; internal affairs units; peer support teams; district attorneys; investigators; city, town, or county counsel; personal attorneys; city, town, or county politicians; the media; and others. Potentially involved parties may benefit from establishing locally acceptable procedures and protocols on handling these stressful, high-profile events to avoid conflict among the many different interests. Continued regular communication will help ensure smooth functioning and necessary adjustments.

Recommendations for Post-shooting Interventions by a Mental Health Professional

20. A post-shooting intervention should be conducted by a licensed mental health professional trained to work with law enforcement personnel. Care should be taken in selecting a mental health professional to ensure that he or she has a strong educational background, knowledge, and experience in the treatment of trauma, and a full spectrum of clinical experience with law enforcement in all types of mental health issues. The credentials and experience of the mental health professional are crucial in conducting post-shooting interventions. Law enforcement administrators are encouraged to examine the mental health professional's background for training and experience with interventions in a law enforcement setting.

21. The initial post-shooting intervention should occur within one week after the shooting incident. The initial goal should be to reduce arousal and provide an opportunity for education and support. Your mental health professional may wish to break up an initial contact to provide information first, and then make a contact later to help the officer process what happened during the shooting. Other experienced police mental health professionals prefer an integrated contact initially.

22. Each agency must decide if the post-shooting intervention will be voluntary or mandatory. Despite progress in the

recognition of the place of mental health professionals in the field of law enforcement, many officers would still decline to participate if post-shooting interventions were offered solely on a voluntary basis. If the post-shooting intervention is mandatory and part of the standard operating procedure, this may help reduce the stigma of seeking help for the officer involved. However, voluntary interventions can reduce resentment and leave an officer feeling more in control at a time when the officer may feel he or she has lost control over what happens to him or her. An alternative is to require that an officer report to the department mental health professional and obtain any information or education that is available, but leaving the officer the option to participate, postpone or decline any intervention that requires sharing his or her personal experience. People reach the point of wanting to process an emotional experience at different times after an event. This can be dependent on other events and activities in an officer's life, the previous experiences with emotionally arousing events, or the individual's personal survival strategy and emotional defenses.

23. It is recommended that post-shooting interventions be done during on-duty time.

24. A single contact with a mental health professional may prove to be inadequate for officers who have been severely affected by an event. Also, a subset of officers may experience delayed onset of problems. Follow-up sessions should be made available to every officer involved.

25. It should also be made clear that the post-shooting intervention is a privileged communication between the mental health professional and the officer involved. There should never be an attempt to gain information about what is said in these sessions by anyone without the permission of the officer.

26. During the post-shooting intervention, there are numerous opportunities for the mental health professional to screen for unusual circumstances (past or present) that could intensify the impact of this particular incident on the officer. The mental health professional should also informally assess, for the sole purpose of voluntary referral, which officers may need additional or alternative types of assistance as part of

their recovery process. If appropriate, referrals should then be offered to chaplains programs, peer support programs, additional counseling, and so on. Much of the time, the normalization process during the post-shooting intervention provides sufficient support to facilitate individual coping mechanisms. Frequently, after a life-threatening incident, officers are most concerned about how they reacted physiologically and emotionally, and whether these reactions were normal. Receiving reassurance during the post-shooting intervention frequently reduces worry, anxiety, and negative self-assessment. If not addressed, these reactions can frequently lead to more severe and chronic problems, and the need for treatment oriented services.

27. All interventions that did not lead to ongoing contacts with the mental health professional should have follow-up contact or a phone call from the mental health professional within four months.

28. Opportunities for a conjoint or family counseling session with the spouse, children, or significant others should be made available when appropriate.

29. It should be made clear to all involved personnel and their supervisors that post-shooting interventions are separate and distinct from any fitness-for-duty assessments or administrative or investigative procedures. This does not preclude a supervisor from requesting a formal fitness-for-duty evaluation based upon concerns about the officer's ability to perform his or her job due to emotional or psychological issues. However, the mere fact of being involved in a shooting does not necessitate such an evaluation prior to return to duty.

30. If a fitness-for-duty evaluation is required, it should not be provided by the mental health professional who did a post-shooting intervention with the officer. A department may choose to enlist the mental health professional who did the post-shooting intervention to help the officer make decisions about returning to duty. In that situation, the department must understand the officer has the right to privilege and confidentiality for anything said in the session that does not pose an imminent threat to self or others.

31. In large-scale operations or incidents, group interventions may be beneficial. It is essential that the groups be screened so they contain individuals who responded to the same event, and that individual counseling referrals be available for those needing or wanting additional assistance. It is often not advisable for the primary officers (those who discharged their weapons) to be included in groups unless they truly desire it. The mental health professional and department administrators should consider legal ramifications caused by the changes in confidentiality and privilege that occur when information is processed in group settings. Legal considerations will vary from state to state.

(Ratified by the IACP Police Psychological Services Section, Los Angeles, California, 2004.)

Peer Support Guidelines

Philosophy

1. The goal of peer support is to provide all public safety employees within an agency the opportunity to receive emotional and tangible peer support through times of personal or professional crises and to help anticipate and address potential difficulties. A peer support program must have a procedure for mental health consultation and training. A peer support program is developed and implemented under the organizational structure of the parent agency.

2. To ensure maximum utilization of the program and to support assurances of confidentiality, there should be participation on the steering committee by relevant employee organizations, mental health professionals, and police administrators during planning and subsequent stages. Membership on the steering committee should have a wide representation of involved sworn and non-sworn parties.

3. Sworn peer support officers are officers first and peer supporters second. Any conflicts of roles should be resolved in that context.

4. A Peer Support Person (PSP), sworn or non-sworn, is a specifically trained colleague, not a counselor or therapist. A peer support program can augment outreach programs, for

example, employee assistance programs and in-house treatment programs, but not replace them. PSPs should refer cases that require professional intervention to a mental health professional. A procedure should be in place for mental health consultations and training.

5. It is beneficial for PSPs to be involved in supporting individuals involved in a critical incident such as an officer-involved shooting. PSPs also make an invaluable addition to group debriefings in conjunction with a licensed mental health professional. However, the IACP Police Psychological Services Section's Officer-Involved Shooting Guidelines recommend that a confidential post-shooting individual debriefing should be conducted by a licensed mental health professional.

Selection

6. PSPs should be chosen from volunteers who are currently in good standing with their departments and who have received recommendations from their superiors and/or peers.

7. Considerations for selection of PSP candidates include, but are not limited to, previous education and training; resolved traumatic experiences; and desirable personal qualities, such as maturity, judgment, and personal and professional credibility.

8. A procedure should be in place that establishes criteria for de-selection from the program. Possible criteria include breach of confidentiality; failure to attend training; or losing one's good standing with the department. PSPs should also be provided with the option to take a leave of absence and encouraged to exercise this option, should personal issues or obligations require it.

Training

9. Relevant introductory and continuing training for a PSP could include the following:
   - Confidentiality Issues
   - Communication Facilitation and Listening Skills

- Ethical Issues
- Problem Assessment
- Problem-Solving Skills
- Alcohol and Substance Abuse
- Cross-Cultural Issues
- Medical Conditions Often Confused with Psychiatric Disorders
- Stress Management
- AIDS Information
- Suicide Assessment
- Depression and Burn-Out
- Grief Management
- Domestic Violence
- Crisis Management
- Nonverbal Communication
- When to Seek Mental Health Consultation and Referral Information
- Traumatic Intervention
- Limits and Liability

Administration

10. A formal policy statement should be included in the departmental policy manual that gives written assurances that, within limits of confidentiality, PSPs will not be asked to give information about members they support. The only information that management may require about peer support cases is the anonymous statistical information regarding the utilization of a PSP.

11. A peer support program shall be governed by a written procedures manual that is available to all personnel.

12. Individuals receiving peer support may voluntarily choose or reject a PSP by using any criteria they believe are important.

13. Management could provide non- compensatory support for the PSP program.

14. Departments are encouraged to train as many employees as possible in peer support skills.

15. A peer support program coordinator should be identified who has a block of time devoted to program logistics and

development. This individual would coordinate referrals to mental health professionals, collect utilization data, and coordinate training and meetings.

16. The peer support program is not an alternative to discipline. A PSP does not intervene in the disciplinary process, even at a member's request.

17. The steering committee shall identify appropriate ongoing training for PSPs.

Consultation Services From Mental Health Professionals

18. PSPs must have a mental health professional with whom to consult. Ideally, this consultation would be available 24 hours a day.

19. PSPs should be aware of their personal limitations and should seek advice and counsel in determining when to disqualify themselves from working with problems for which they have not been trained or problems about which they may have strong personal beliefs.

20. PSPs should be required to advance their skills through continuing training as scheduled by the program coordinator.

Confidentiality

21. PSPs must inform department members of the limits of their confidentiality and consider potential role conflicts (e.g., supervisor providing peer support). These should be consistent with the law as well as departmental policy and may include the following:

- Threats to self
- Threats to specific people
- Felonies as specified by the department
- Serious misdemeanors as specified by the department
- Child, spouse, and elder abuse

22. PSPs should be trained to be sensitive to role conflicts that could affect future decisions or recommendations concerning assignment, transfer, or promotion. PSPs cannot abdicate

their job responsibility as officers by participating in the program.

23. PSPs must not volunteer information to supervisors and should advise supervisors of the confidentiality guidelines established by the department.

24. PSPs must advise members that information told to them is not protected by legal privilege and that confidentiality is administratively provided and may not be recognized in court proceedings.

25. PSPs should avoid conflicting peer support relationships. For example, PSPs should not develop peer support relationships with supervisors, subordinates, or relatives. PSPs should avoid religious, sexual, or financial entanglements with receivers of peer support and avoid espousing particular values, moral standards, and philosophies.

26. A PSP must not keep written formal or private records of supportive contacts.

(Ratified by the IACP Police Psychological Services Section, Los Angeles, California, 2004.)

In the Appendix for this chapter, the International Association of Chiefs of Police Psychological Evaluation Guidelines has also been included.

Summary

The goal of psychological screening is to eliminate high-risk candidates while withstanding legal challenges and complying with civil mandates.

Psychological testing is one tool that can be used as part of a larger screening process to accomplish this in a reliable way. While the psychological test should not be a single determinant, it can confirm or refute information received in other segments of the selection process.

The community deserves a complete selection process, including a psychological process that includes both written testing and an interview with a licensed psychologist knowledgeable in law enforcement issues. The psychologist should be experienced in working specifically with law enforcement personnel, so that he or she understands the wide variety of specific requirements and responsibilities that make up the job tasks of an officer.

It is also important that the psychological testing process include a face-to-face interview in addition to written testing. The purpose of the post-test psychological interview is to verify the information that has been obtained through the psychological testing process, and to gain the additional insight of the psychologist on whether or not the candidate is appropriate for such a sensitive position. In addition, this meeting can act as a debriefing for the candidates, allowing them the opportunity to ask questions and to better understand themselves.

Predicting behavior is always difficult, and requires a complete screening process to be successful. The law enforcement officer is required to have the ability to survive a life and death struggle, yet be compassionate on a consistent basis without room for error. While future behavior cannot be predicted exactly, the psychological testing process can provide a sound basis for alerting an agency of potential problems. When properly documented with an awareness of potential challenges, it can also serve to defend the selection process in subsequent litigation.

Appendix 17-1
Pre-Employment Psychological Evaluation Guidelines

(Ratified by the IACP Police Psychological Services Section Denver, Colorado, 2009.)

1. Purpose

1.1. The IACP Police Psychological Services Section developed these guidelines for use by public safety agencies and individuals who are charged with the responsibility of conducting defensible pre-employment psychological evaluation programs.

2. Limitations

2.1. These guidelines are not intended to establish a rigid standard of practice for pre-employment psychological evaluations. Instead, they are intended to reflect the commonly accepted practices of the Section members and the agencies they serve.

2.2. Each of the guidelines may not apply in a specific case or in all situations. The decision as to what is or is not done in a particular instance is ultimately the responsibility of each hiring agency and psychologist.

2.3. Nothing in these guidelines should be construed to discourage scientific research, innovation, and/or use of new techniques that show promise for helping hiring agencies identify, screen, and select qualified candidates. Hiring agencies and psychologists who choose to use these practices may wish to consult with legal counsel to assess the potential liability exposure.

2.4. These guidelines are written to apply to agencies within the jurisdiction of the United States and, as such, may require modification for use by agencies in other countries.

3. Definitions

3.1. For the purpose of these guidelines, a pre-employment psychological evaluation is a specialized examination of an applicant's psychological suitability for a public safety position. These positions include, but are not limited to, positions where incumbents have arrest authority or the legal authority to detain and confine individuals.

3.2. Psychological suitability includes, at a minimum, the absence of job-relevant mental or emotional conditions that would reasonably be expected to interfere with safe and effective performance.

3.3. Under the terms of the Americans with Disabilities Act (ADA) a procedure or test that seeks information about an individual's physical or mental impairments or health, or that provides evidence that would lead to identifying a mental disorder or impairment, is a "medical examination." Therefore, a pre-employment psychological evaluation constitutes a medical examination.

3.4. A pre-employment psychological evaluation may include procedures or tests that are not medical in nature (i.e., designed and used to measure personality traits, behaviors, or characteristics such as judgment, stress resilience, anger management, integrity, conscientiousness, teamwork, social competence). However, these non-medical procedures alone would not constitute a complete pre-employment psychological evaluation since they do not include the required elements specified in 3.2 and 3.3.

3.5. The ADA plays an important role in the timing of when the evaluation can be performed in the hiring process. Under the ADA, the use of medical inquiries or examinations may occur only after (a) the hiring agency has obtained and analyzed all relevant non-medical information that it reasonably could have obtained and analyzed, and (b) the applicant has been given a conditional offer of employment.

4.   Examiner Qualifications

4.1. Evaluations should be conducted by licensed doctoral-level psychologists, except where otherwise permitted by law, with expertise in clinical psychological testing and assessment, as well as in personnel evaluation using measures of normal personality characteristics, skills and abilities. Psychologists should also be trained and experienced in psychological evaluations for public safety positions, in particular.

4.2. Psychologists should be familiar with the research literature available on psychological testing for public safety positions. Psychologists should also be familiar with employment law impacting the conduct of pre-employment psychological evaluations, including but not limited to the ADA, or other federal and state laws applicable to the practitioner's jurisdiction. Psychologists should consult with legal counsel when appropriate.

4.3. Psychologists must adhere to ethical principles and standards for practice in their jurisdiction.

5. Job Analysis

5.1. Information about duties, powers, demands, working conditions, and other job-analytic information relevant to the intended position, should be obtained by the psychologist before beginning the evaluation process. This information should be directed toward identifying behaviors and attributes that underlie effective and counterproductive job performance.

5.2. The psychologist should consult with the hiring agency to establish selection criteria and the agency's level of acceptable risk for problematic behaviors.

6. Disclosure

6.1. Prior to the administration of any psychological instruments and interview, the psychologist and/or hiring agency should disclose information to the applicant that includes: (1) the nature and objectives of the evaluation, (2) the intended recipients, (3) that the hiring agency is the client, (4) the probable uses of the evaluation and the information obtained, (5) who will have access to the information, and (6) the limits of confidentiality.

6.2. The disclosure should be documented in writing and signed by the applicant.

7. Testing

7.1. Use: A written test battery, including objective, job-related psychological assessment instruments, should be administered to the applicant. Test results should be available to the evaluator before the interview is conducted.

7.1.1. The licensed psychologist should always retain responsibility to verify and interpret all psychological test results.

7.1.2. Tests should be administered, scored, and interpreted according to the publisher's recommendations and consistent with established test administration standards.

7.1.3. Test scales, profiles and reports used for selection purposes should be produced using appropriate, current software or scoring keys licensed by the publisher of the test.

7.2. Validity: Written assessment instruments should have validation evidence for use with public safety applicants.

7.2.1. Tests should have a substantial research base for interpretation with normal range populations in general, and public safety applicants in particular. Validation evidence should be consistent with Principles for the Validation and Use of Personnel Selection Procedures.

7.2.2. Specific cut-off scores should be used only when there is adequate statistical evidence that such scores are predictive of personality or mental health problems that are detrimental to job performance. If cut-off scores are used, the psychologist should acknowledge their use and be prepared to provide the justification for using the specific cut-off level.

7.2.3. New or emerging psychological instruments may be added to a battery to develop the requisite norms and validation, but should not be used for decision-making by the evaluating psychologist during the data-gathering process.

7.3. Security: The psychologist should make provisions for the security and confidentiality of all testing materials (e.g., test booklets/items) including materials presented electronically. Provisions should also be made for the security of, access to, and retention of the psychological reports and raw data, including information stored or transmitted electronically.

8. Interview

8.1. Individual, face-to-face interviews with applicants should be conducted before a final determination of the applicant's psychological suitability is made.

8.2. A semi-structured, job-related interview format should be employed with all applicants.

8.3. Interviews should allow for sufficient time to cover appropriate background, test results verification and clinical assessment.

9. Background Information

9.1. Information regarding the applicant's relevant history (e.g., school, work, interpersonal, family, legal, financial, substance use, mental health) should be collected and integrated with psychological test and interview data. When available, relevant information from the background investigation and polygraph examination should be shared with the psychologist.

9.2. If relevant to psychological suitability, health records should be obtained from treating healthcare professional(s) for review before a final determination is made of the applicant's suitability. When such records are unavailable, consideration should be given to deferring the suitability determination until the health record can be reviewed or the basis for the concern is otherwise resolved.

9.3. When background investigation findings are not provided to the psychologist in advance of the evaluation, it is desirable for the psychologist to communicate with designated hiring agency staff, prior to making a final suitability determination, to compare and reconcile information obtained from the applicant. In all cases, substantive discrepancies between information obtained in the psychological evaluation and other stages of the hiring process should be reviewed thoroughly with the hiring agency before a final hiring decision is made.

10. Reports

10.1. The hiring agency administrators directly involved in making employment decisions should be provided with a written report of the psychologist's evaluation. The report should contain, at a minimum, a clear determination of the applicant's psychological suitability for employment based upon an analysis of all psychological assessment material, including background information, test data, and interview. Any agency-specific restrictions or other requirements relevant to the format or content of the psychological report should be communicated to the psychologist in advance of the evaluation.

10.2. Ratings and/or recommendations for employment based on the results of the evaluation should be expressly linked to the job-analytic information referenced in paragraphs 5.1 and 5.2.

10.3. While a clinical assessment of overall psychological suitability should be made, clinical diagnoses or psychiatric labeling of applicants should be avoided unless relevant to the psychologist's conclusion, necessary for the hiring agency to make an employment decision, and/or required by law. In all cases, the evaluation should be focused on an individual applicant's ability to safely and effectively perform the essential functions of the position under consideration.

10.4. Conclusions concerning an applicant's qualifications should be based generally on consistencies across data sources rather than a single source; psychologists should justify exceptions to this guideline.

10.5. Additional information, including ratings, recommendations, justifications for the recommendation and/or rating, reservations that the psychologist might have regarding the validity or reliability of the results, and other elements required by law in the hiring agency's jurisdiction, should be disclosed on a need-to-know basis, in consultation with the hiring authority.

10.6. The report should clearly state the period of time for which the evaluation is considered valid. In the absence of a legally prescribed limitation, reports should be valid for no longer than one year from completion of the evaluation.

10.7. The written report provided to the agency should be securely maintained in accordance with applicable regulations.

11. Use of the Evaluation

11.1. Efforts should be made to inform the hiring agency's administrators about the strengths and limitations of pre-employment psychological evaluations.

11.2. Pre-employment psychological evaluations should be used as one component of the overall hiring process.

11.3. Care should be taken when using pre-employment test results for purposes other than making pre-employment decisions.

11.4. The hiring agency should not use the pre-employment evaluation for promotional evaluations or for positions not expressly considered by the psychologist at the time of the evaluation.

12. Follow-up

12.1. Continuing collaborative efforts by the hiring agency and evaluating psychologist should be made to assess the accuracy of the final suitability determination. Follow-up data should be collected in accordance with strict confidentiality provisions protecting individual applicant identities and in accordance with ethical research guidelines and the law.

12.2. The psychologist and/or hiring agency should evaluate whether final suitability ratings have an adverse impact on protected classes of candidates.

12.3. Psychologists should be prepared to defend their procedures, conclusions, and recommendations if a decision based on psychological evaluation results is challenged.

13. Appeals and Second Opinions

13.1. Hiring agencies that permit second-opinion evaluations as part of an appeal process should require that these psychological evaluations be based upon the same criteria used for the initial psychological evaluation.

References

5.1 - Please see the Equal Employment Opportunity Commission's Enforcement Guidance, ADA Enforcement Guidance: Pre-employment Disability-Related Questions and Medical Examinations, at www.eeoc.gov/policy/docs/preemp.html.

7.2.2 - Please see the Principles for the Validation and Use of Personnel Selection Procedures, 4th Edition, August 2003, at http://www.siop.org/_Principles/principles.pdf

Recommendations and Key Points for a Psychological Examination

The following recommendations are made concerning psychological examination of law enforcement candidates:

1. Psychological testing should be used to reduce liability to law enforcement agencies. Damage awards have been granted against law enforcement agencies that have failed to screen out unsuitable candidates.
2. Psychological testing should evaluate the potential emotional stability of an officer candidate for law enforcement service. This emotional stability must be measured against essential job functions.
3. Psychologists cannot foresee the future emotional potential of a candidate. However, the administration of sound psychological testing can help identify candidates suitable for law enforcement service.
4. The goal of psychological screening is to eliminate high-risk candidates while withstanding legal challenges and complying with civil mandates.
5. Both formal and informal efforts should be made to clarify the goals of psychological testing for law enforcement candidates.
6. A rating system for evaluation should be developed that provides for more than a "yes" or a "no" response in determination of the candidate's psychological stability.
7. Psychologists conducting screenings should be familiar not only with the psychological testing for law enforcement officers, but should also be knowledgeable about law enforcement officers and their job functions.
8. Written psychological tests should be validated for use with law enforcement candidates, and the selected tests should avoid adverse impact based on sex and race.
9. The psychological testing process should include both a written test and an interview with a licensed psychologist.
10. It is recommended that the IACP guidelines regarding the use of psychological services be followed by all law enforcement agencies for psychological testing of applicants.
11. A psychological FFDE is a formal, specialized examination of an incumbent employee that results from (1) objective evidence that the employee may be unable to safely or effectively perform a

defined job and (2) a reasonable basis for believing that the cause may be attributable to psychological factors.

12. The central purpose of an FFDE is to determine whether the employee is able to safely and effectively perform his or her essential job functions.

References

Marzella, J. Nick, Ph.D.; "Psychological screening: to Test or not to test? Is that the question?", The *Ohio Police Chief Magazine*, July 2000.

American Psychological Association, Washington D.C.; "Standards for psychological screening of police officers" from: Inwald, Robin and Jody Resko. "Pre-employment Screening for Public Safety Personnel" Innovations in Clinical Practice, A Source Book, Vol. XIV.

International Association of Chiefs of Police. (September 2005). The Police Chief, Vol. 72, No. 9. Alexandria, VA.

Chapter 18

Medical Examination

Introduction

It cannot be argued that the most expensive investment of any organization is in its personnel. The importance of personnel allocation begins with the initial hiring process. The necessity of including medical examinations in the hiring process should not be discounted, nor should organizations short change themselves by not providing comprehensive medical examinations to its candidates. To do so can be a costly oversight in the long run, in terms of personnel costs.

In determining the qualifications of candidates for any type of position, employers look at educational background, personal abilities and skills, previous experience, and moral standing. While all of these contribute to the selection process, the issue of a potential employee's medical condition is extremely important. With the costs associated in the selection process, necessary on-the-job training and retention, and equipping the employee, an entity cannot afford to make a serious mistake by not looking closely at the ability of the potential employee to stay healthy and be a productive resource for the organization.

There is also the cost of lost time due to absenteeism to be considered when reviewing the need for a complete medical examination of a potential employee. Lost time in terms of absenteeism due to sick leave, including the possibility of overtime costs to cover for absent employees, is a very real drain on any agency's budget. Insurance costs due to rising medical expenditures and Workers' Compensation benefits are additional costs. Add to this the intangible costs of other employees' morale when they are required to work additional hours or have requested leave turned down, and the full picture of associated cost in hiring a person with potential medical issues becomes clearer.

With this said, what then should a medical examination include? What needs to be excluded due to privacy issues and how do federal guidelines and laws, such as the Americans with Disabilities Act, affect what an agency can and cannot do in this area? Let us examine these issues individually.

What Should Be Included in a Thorough Medical Examination?

The state of Ohio will be used as an example of how medical examinations may be administered to ensure that officers hired do not have pre-existing medical conditions that might be aggravated by performing essential job functions.

As with any pre-employment testing procedure, the medical examination must follow the established legal guidelines set by the state in which the agency operates, as well as the federal guidelines of the Americans with Disabilities Act. More on this will follow. Within the State of Ohio, there now exists minimum medical testing and diagnostic procedures established under House Bill 648, which was enacted in 1998. The purpose of these minimum guidelines is to assist in evaluating a candidate's potential pre-existing medical condition as it relates to heart, cardiovascular, and respiratory diseases. Unless evidence of these diseases is revealed in a pre-employment examination or other competent evidence is available, these conditions are presumed by law to have been incurred in the performance of an officer's official duties.

For this reason, the Police and Firemen's Disability and Pension Fund of Ohio now requires specific testing prior to qualifying a police officer or firefighter for the pension system. Under Section 742.38 of the Ohio Revised Code and Section 742-1-02 of the Ohio Administrative Code, the agency/governmental entity of candidates entitled to benefits under the Police and Firemen's Disability and Pension Fund must file a physician's report with the Pension Fund that certifies certain testing has been completed on a Pension Fund applicant.

Those tests that must be administered by a licensed physician within the State of Ohio and certified include:

- A medical questionnaire that includes past medical history, family history, and occupational history;
- An actual physical examination of the candidate;
- Medical testing to include:

  1. Spirometry that represents at least a valid and reproducible forced expiratory volume at one (1) second

(FEVI), forced vital capacity (FVC), and forced expiratory volume at one (1) second/forced vital capacity (FEVI/FVC) that meets the criteria of the American Thoracic Society;

2. A chest x-ray that is at least a P.A. 72" (i.e. front to back);
3. Lipid profile that includes cholesterol (both LDL and HDL);
4. An electrocardiogram (EKG) and cardiac stress test performed consistent with standard Bruce protocol.
   i. Diagnoses/conclusions of identified and past conditions;
   ii. Diagnoses and evaluation of the existence of any heart disease, cardiovascular disease, or respiratory disease identified in any of the questionnaire, medical tests, and physical examination required.

The Pension Fund also provides to the agency a copy of the U.S. Department of Labor's occupational characteristics and vocational preparation for physical demands of public safety occupations.

It should be clear from the information now being requested by state regulations and the Pension Board covering the majority of municipal police officers and firefighters within the State of Ohio, that medical examinations must be thorough not only in rudimentary application but also in the general cardiopulmonary condition of an applicant.

To anyone who has been actively engaged in the law enforcement profession, it is fairly safe to say that heart attacks are known to be a major contributor of disability claims in this occupation. Research has noted that police officers, at least in the past, have been susceptible to heart disease due to the stress of the job, poor eating habits, sedentary working conditions that are spiked by moments of extreme physical requirements, duress and adrenalin, and smoking habits. It can certainly be reasoned that a thorough medical examination is a cost-effective issue from the standpoint of job performance and future insurance costs to the entity. Job demands require that potential candidates have the physical capacity to perform, especially under stress. A thorough medical examination is one way of assessing such capacity of a candidate.

As with any pre-employment testing device, the medical examination must be job related and verifiable. Developing physical capacity standards must comply with the Americans with Disabilities Act of 1990 and the Civil Rights Act of 1991.

"These statutes place the burden of identifying the essential functions of a job, including physical requirements, on the employer. They also prohibit special treatment for job candidates beyond a fair and equal opportunity to compete for a job. These federal laws, and associated local statutes, require that any information used to determine employment be based only on actual job requirements. The development of physical capacity standards permit the hiring of only those candidates who demonstrate they have the physical capacity to do the job. Such workers begin employment with the greatest chance of long-term success. Fit individuals not only tend to be injured less often, but their injuries are generally less severe and recovery is rapid. All of these factors have a positive effect on medical and lost time costs." [1] Therefore, testing must be precise in measuring quantifiable characteristics. It must be bias-free with regard to gender, ethnicity, race, and to some degree age (the age requirement for candidates is a matter of jurisdictional review). The testing mechanism must be reliable, and this is attained by having the testing administered by a certified, licensed physician, or occupational health center.

Testing for job relatedness demonstrates the candidate can perform the necessary functions of the job (occupational characteristics). Defining job related physical standards begins with developing a Job Task Analysis of the assigned position. The purpose of a Job Task Analysis is to document the essential physical requirements of a job. "Job descriptions, standards, operating procedures, collective bargaining agreements, and other documentation that determine what and how work is performed should be reviewed to define essential job tasks, performance parameters and any physical demands." [2]

---

[1]   O'Conner, John S.; Warner, Carlene "How to Develop Physical Capacity Standards," *Personnel Journal* May 96, vol. 75 Issue 5.

[2]   "How to Develop Physical Capacity Standards," *Personnel Journal*, May 96.

When Should the Medical Examination Be Given?

The Americans with Disabilities Act requires that employers not ask a candidate about past or present medical conditions or workers' compensation injuries until after making a conditional job offer to that applicant. There is case law on this, *Steeltek, Inc. vs. Griffin, US. No. 981194* being one notable example.[1] However, upon completion of all pre-employment screening and a medical evaluation, an employer may legally not hire an applicant if:

1. It can be shown the applicant lied.
2. A medical evaluation (including a psychological examination) determines the applicant is a safety or health risk to him/herself or others.
3. A medical evaluation determines the applicant is unable to perform the essential functions of the job.
4. A conditional offer may be withdrawn if a background check finds denial of multiple Workers' Compensation claims, which may indicate potential fraud.[2]

It is important to document what is a conditional job offer to most thoroughly evaluate a candidate's medical condition prior to actually starting on the job. A guide is available from the Equal Employment Opportunity Commission (EEOC) providing clarification of what constitutes post-employment medical examinations and inquiries. The "Enforcement Guidance of Pre-employment Disability-related Inquiries and Medical Examinations Under the Americans with Disabilities Act" gives definitions of important language and provides examples of tests and analyses by which agencies can test their compliance.

The guide defines "bona fide offer" as, "an act that reasonably leads the offeree to believe that a power to create a contract has been conferred on him." Further, to be considered a bona fide offer, the

---

[1] Limits of Pre-Employment Inquiries under ADA" (Hatch, D. Diana; Hall, James E., Workforce, July 99 Vol. 78).

[2] "Making Pre-Employment Screening Work," Fletcher, Meg, Business Insurance, Nov. 97, p. 91.

agency should have evaluated all relevant non-medical information that could reasonably have been analyzed prior to the offers.[1]

In summary, the recommended time for a full and complete medical examination is after a bona fide conditional job offer has been made. Further, the EEOC guidelines caution that the employer must have evaluated all non-medical information that, from a practical and legal perspective, could reasonably have been analyzed prior to extending the job offer. If an examination or medical inquiry screens out an individual with a disability, the employer must demonstrate that the rejection is job related and consistent with the position being applied for.

Medical Examinations and the ADA

For the purposes of the Americans with Disabilities Act (ADA) of 1990, medical examinations are those tests and/or analyses performed by a health care professional, which measure the existence, nature, and severity of a person's physical or mental health and the identification of any physical or psychological impairment. Agencies need not worry about constraints from ADA as long as the medical examinations performed are job related and the more in-depth questioning of previous or current potential medical concerns are presented to a candidate after a bona fide job offer has been made.

It is important to also note the difference between health issues and physical ability issues. Medical examinations will concern themselves with the overall health status of an applicant. Agencies interested in the physical abilities of a candidate should look at physical capacity or fitness standards such as the Cooper Institute testing mechanisms. A candidate's relative strength, flexibility, and endurance are not usually measured by a medical examination. This is not to say that physical capacity parameters cannot be converted to physiological requirements. As noted earlier, this is an area where job-task analysis and performance requirements for the job play an important part in the overall measurement of physical ability.

---

[1] "Post-employment Medical Examinations and Inquiries Clarified" (Schneid, Thomas D., *Fire Engineering*, June 96, Vol. 149, Issue 6, p.120. 6 Risk Management, Fish, Marilyn M., April, 1997).

Agencies must also consider whether an applicant could perform the tasks of a job if given reasonable accommodations to assist in the performance of those tasks at question. However, an entity need not provide accommodations if doing so would create undue hardships on the operations of that entity. This is, of course, an extremely litigious determination and should be made only after consultation with legal representatives knowledgeable in ADA standards.

Drug Screening as Part of the Medical Examination

Drug screening of candidates is legal as long as it is done uniformly and consistent to established guidelines so as to rule out potential claims of discrimination and bias in employment opportunities. Again, the ADA requirements are that drug screening be administered after a conditional job offer has been extended.

According to a study conducted by RTW, Inc. on average, 15 percent of American workers are substance abusers, and are three to four times as likely to suffer injury on the job.[1] Within law enforcement, drug usage of any type was once an almost certain disqualifier for police candidates. Since the 1970s and an emergence of a more relaxed social consideration of "soft" drug experimentation, more police departments have had to pare down their drug usage restrictions in order to meet the demand for otherwise qualified workers in an increasingly competitive job market.

Studies are not conclusive; however, there can be a reasonable expectation that a drug-free workplace would have a less likely percentage of injury related Workers Compensation claims than a workplace with limited or no checks on drug usage of employees.

Summary

Agencies today use or, at least, have variety of screening applications available to them in order to determine the best candidates for highly competitive job considerations. The medical examination is but one tool, however, it can arguably be considered the most important tool in the screening process. While background checks may uncover areas of medical concerns that an agency would

---

[1] "Survey: Medical Testing of a job applicant lowers costs": Goch, Lynna, *Best's Review*, July, 99.

want to check out, it is the medical examination itself that will provide the necessary documentation of acceptable or unacceptable medical concerns.

In an effort to control the ever increasing cost of health care for employees, government agencies, as well as private businesses, would short change themselves if they did not include some safeguards in the physical and mental condition of candidates prior to actually putting them to work. Such short sightedness would have both short- and long-term consequences in the form of potential sick leave and absenteeism, Workers Compensation claims, high insurance costs, and disability claims, and morale issues among the workforce.

Recommendations and Key Points for a Medical Examination

The following recommendations are made concerning medical examination of law enforcement candidates:

1. Medical examinations help select healthy employees and avoid absenteeism due to sick leave, which potentially lowers overtime costs.
2. Medical examinations help lower the government agency's rising insurance and Workers Compensation costs by selecting healthier employees.
3. The Ohio Police and Firemen's Disability and Pension Fund of Ohio requires specific testing prior to qualifying a police officer, and filing this physician's report with the Pension Fund.
4. Fit individuals tend not only to be injured less often, but their injuries are generally less severe and recovery is more rapid.
5. The medical examination must be job related and verifiable.
6. The Americans with Disabilities Act of 1990 and The Civil Rights Act of 1991 place the burden of identifying essential functions of a job, including physical requirements, on the employer.
7. Defining job-related physical standards begins with developing a job-task analysis of the assigned position.

8. Medical examinations should be conducted only after a conditional job offer to evaluate the candidate's medical condition prior to actually starting on the job.

9. If a medical examination screens out an individual with a disability, the employer must demonstrate that the rejection is job related and consistent with the job.

10. Drug screening is permissible as long as it is done legally and uniformly.

Chapter 19

Legal Considerations for Entry-Level Hiring

Introduction

Pre-employment interviewing is perhaps the most important tool in the hiring process. During a face-to-face interview, the employer is provided the opportunity to observe and evaluate the appearance of the applicant and directly review previously provided information pertaining to the applicant and the position.

Although an integral aspect of the hiring process, pre-employment interviewing is not without the potential for employer liability. Pre-employment interviewing involves legal pitfalls that the employers performing the interview must consider. Applicants are garnered various protections by both state and federal law. Because of laws such as the American with Disabilities Act (ADA), the Age Discrimination in Employment Act (ADEA), Title VII and the Ohio Civil Rights Act, employers must proceed cautiously and be cognizant of question topics to avoid while conducting a thorough, productive, and legal hiring process. These, many times, must be considered in conjunction with the civil service process.

Illegal Questions When Interviewing

Although the following discussion pertains largely to legal considerations for employers during the interview process, the areas of questioning to avoid are not limited solely to the face-to-face interview. Employers must avoid asking illegal questions or seeking illegal information during the application process, as well. Generally, topics of questions to avoid during the interview and application process include questions relating to:

- Race
- National Origin
- Sex
- Marital Status
- Pregnancy

- Child Care
- Age
- Religion
- Arrests and Convictions
- Friends and Relatives
- Disability Discrimination

The focus of interview questions must be: Are you able to perform the essential function of this job — with or without reasonable accommodations? The above list is by no means exhaustive and should not serve as an automatic disqualifier for discussion or inquiry about a particular topic. Certain rules or exceptions may apply in the area of law enforcement.

Further, at the outset it must be noted that the following rules, laws, and procedures apply to any outside firms retained to complete the hiring process. The city or the police agency may be liable for any errors or illegal inquiry committed by the outside agency conducting the hiring process. Thus, a law enforcement department opting to contract-out the hiring process must closely observe the hiring procedure to ensure that the outside firm is in compliance with the law.

General Information Concerning Civil Service Law

The legal considerations of entry level hiring for a law enforcement agency goes beyond general considerations as to what type of information can be sought and obtained. The initial consideration of a department must be "how is the vacant position to be filled?" In other words, must the vacancy be filled pursuant to "Civil Service Law," the city charter, or a collective bargaining agreement. Additionally, police departments must act in close coordination with their respective city Civil Service Commissions, if applicable. Although hiring of law enforcement personnel may be generally governed by state law, city Civil Service Commissions may have enacted specific rules governing the of hiring new employees. If a city Civil Service Commission has enacted its own civil service rules, then the city's civil service rules govern the hiring process. Further, instances may exist in which a city Civil Service Commission delegates to the city police department the authority to govern its hiring procedures. Because of the intricacies and interplay between the state law and city Civil Service rules, it is essential that a city police department be aware of both the governing rules and the necessary procedure for filling a vacancy.

Civil Service Laws

The fundamental purpose of civil service laws and civil service rules is to secure maximum efficiency and integrity in public service by removing the taint of the political spoils system and to shield employees from the pressures of the political system. Civil service laws establish a merit system whereby selections for appointments and promotions in public service may be made on the basis of demonstrated relative fitness and competence, thereby safeguarding appointees from unjust charges of misconduct and inefficiency and the potentially unscrupulous whims of their appointing authorities. The merit system serves to eradicate the spoils system by guaranteeing permanent tenure to persons in the classified service and protecting them from being arbitrarily discharged and replaced with a political appointee.

Classified positions must be filled through competitive examination. Whether a position is classified or unclassified it may be governed by civil service or codified personnel rules. Generally speaking, unclassified positions are at-will, thus termination can occur for any lawful reason. Educational requirements may be imposed where education and training are necessary to the performance of a specific job or professional pursuit. Other inquiries concerning applicant's age, health, and physical ability are governed in part by the ADA and/or ADEA.

As a general rule, the employer should clearly indicate to the applicant the requirements of the position, as well as the procedure that will be utilized.

By clearly indicating the hiring requirements, both the employer and employee will avoid any miscommunication or misunderstanding regarding the position. A clear understanding of the process will result in a more efficient and effective process.

Before taking the examination, reasonable notice of the exam should be given. Reasonable notice includes the time, place, and general scope of the competitive examination. The examination may be used to evaluate one's education, training, knowledge, manual dexterity, and physical and physiological fitness. Potential employees should be notified of all the requirements of the position, at the outset. Again, though, the scope of the examination must be proper within the confines of federal employment laws, such as the ADA.

Because of special exceptions often listed in civil service law for police officers, candidates can be asked very specific, narrowly-tailored questions regarding their age and physical capabilities. However, absent these specific exceptions, the employer must be wary of the information sought on the competitive examination.

Charter Municipalities

Although the hiring of City police officers is typically governed by civil service rules, certain municipalities may be exempt from civil service requirements. Generally, a charter municipality is free to adopt rules regarding appointment and promotion regardless of those rules legislatively mandated by state law. The appointment of officers in police and fire departments represents the exercise of a power of local self-government within a state constitution providing for home rule. In the event of a conflict, charter provisions generally will prevail if they are not inconsistent with the Constitution and if they are specifically expressed in the charter.

Collective Bargaining Agreements

The rules and procedures for filling a vacancy may differ or deviate from civil service rules if the vacant position is within a bargaining unit subject to a collective bargaining agreement. The respective state law will define the parameters of a collective bargaining agreement. Courts have consistently ruled in favor of allowing a collective bargaining agreement to prevail over conflicting provisions in state or local laws, unless specifically exempted by state law. Due to various requirements, it is imperative that an employer follows the necessary procedures for hiring a new employee. A failure to abide by the necessary rules may result in the hiring of an employee being declared improper. Further, employing a wrongfully hired employee may result in liability to the department and the city. The department must also remember that although a city may be exempt from the civil service rules listed under state law and governed by its own rules or agreement, it is still impermissible, improper, and illegal to seek information prohibited by other state and federal laws.

Americans with Disabilities Act of 1990

The Americans with Disabilities Act (ADA) prohibits discrimination against a qualified individual with a disability. The qualified individual with a disability must be able to perform the essential functions of the job with or without reasonable accommodation.

A qualified individual with a disability is an individual who:

1. has a physical or mental impairment that substantially limits a major life activity;
2. has a record of a substantially limiting impairment; or
3. is regarded by the employer as having a substantially limiting impairment.

A substantially limiting impairment to a major life activity results when the disability causes the individual to be unable to perform a major life activity that an average person in the population can perform.

Major life activities include:

- Working;
- Learning;
- Caring for oneself;
- Sitting;
- Performing manual tasks;
- Standing;
- Walking;
- Lifting;
- Seeing;
- Mental and emotional processes such as thinking, concentrating and interacting with others;
- Speaking;
- Breathing

The **essential functions** of the job are the basic job duties that the individual must be able to perform with or without reasonable accommodation. It is critical that the employer establish the essential functions of each classification. The courts have been very supportive of law enforcement's need for higher standards for entry into and maintaining positions in law enforcement. This does not lessen the need for each department and organization to establish valid, defensible essential functions, also commonly referred to as minimal qualifications.

The ADA extends to state and local governments. Therefore, it is improper for law enforcement agencies to discriminate against otherwise qualified applicants who can perform the essential functions of the job with or without reasonable accommodation.

ADA Impact on Pre-employment Inquiries

Because it is unlawful for employers to discriminate against an employee on the basis of a disability, employers must proceed with caution when interviewing applicants. Any question and subsequent answer that may inform the employer of an applicant's disability may result in a claim of disability discrimination should the applicant not be offered a position.

Therefore, in the pre-employment phase of the hiring process it is necessary that the employer refrain from asking questions regarding specific topics. For example, the employer should not ask the applicant about his or her mental conditions, diseases, hospitalization history, major illnesses, physical defects, disabilities, drug prescriptions, treatment for drug addiction or alcoholism, or Workers' Compensation history.

However, the employer may describe the essential functions of the job, including attendance requirements, and ask whether the applicant can perform those functions with or without reasonable accommodation. If the applicant indicates accommodation is required, the employer may then inquire into the nature and extent of the accommodation needed. The employer may also state the attendance requirements of the job and ask how the applicant can meet the attendance requirements.

Additionally, an applicant can be asked to describe and demonstrate how they will perform other non-essential job functions.

However, a decision about the applicant must only be made regarding the ability to perform the essential job functions.

Post-offer Examinations

Post-offer medical examinations are permissible. Further, an offer of employment can be made contingent upon the passing of a medical examination. Post-offer medical examinations must be given to all applicants in the same category that are offered a position. The information garnered from the post-offer medical examination must be kept in a separate place and treated as if it is a confidential medical record. It is considered a confidential record both under the ADA.

Interview Questions and the ADA

Disability-related inquiries are the types of inquiries that will likely invoke the ADA. Disability-related inquiries are inquiries that are likely to elicit information about a disability. However, inquiries about the ability to perform job functions are not disability-related inquiries. The permissible and improper areas of questioning may significantly overlap.

The following examples are inquiries which are not disability related and are permissible:

- Can you perform the functions of this job (essential and/or marginal), with or without reasonable accommodation?
- Please describe/demonstrate how you would perform these functions (essential and/or marginal).
- Can you meet the attendance requirements of this job?
- How many days did you take leave last year?
- Do you have the required licenses to perform this job?
- How much do you weigh?
- How tall are you?
- Do you regularly eat three meals per day?

The following examples are disability-related inquiries that should be avoided during the course of an interview.

- Do you have AIDS?
- Do you have asthma?

- Do you have a disability that would interfere with your ability to perform the job?
- How many days were you sick last year?
- Have you ever filed for Workers' Compensation?
- Have you ever been injured on the job?
- How much alcohol do you drink each week?
- Have you ever been treated for alcohol problems?
- Have you ever been treated for mental health problems?
- What prescription drugs are you currently taking?

Employers must proceed cautiously when inquiring about an applicant's medical or physical qualifications. Employers should not ask questions that would result in the discovery of a disability. Employers can ask questions pertaining to whether the applicant can perform the essential functions of the job with or without reasonable accommodation. However, police departments typically can require applicants to perform physical examination prior to their appointment.

Age Discrimination in Employment Act

Purpose of the ADEA

Generally, the Age Discrimination in Employment Act (ADEA) implements a broad ban against age discrimination. Specifically, the ADEA prohibits the following:

- Statements or specifications in job notices or advertisements of age preference and limitations;
- Discrimination based upon age by apprenticeship programs;
- Denial of benefits to older employees (an employer may reduce benefits based upon age only if the cost of providing the reduced benefits to older employees is the same as the cost of providing benefits to the younger workers).

Exceptions are made to the general prohibitions against age discrimination where an applicant's age is a proven, legitimate bona fide occupational qualification (BFOQ). In other words, if the employee must be a certain age to perform the functions of the position, then age can be a legitimate qualifier. Certain positions within the police department will require a BFOQ.

The age of a candidate to be a police officer is a BFOQ. Some states based on subsequent judicial decisions have determined that it is permissible for a police department to have age requirements for job applicants. For example, provisions in Ohio state law dictates that an applicant for a police department must be twenty-one (21) years old in order to receive an original appointment and the maximum appointment age of an applicant to serve as a police officer may be thirty-five (35) years. The maximum age limitations provided in the Ohio Revised Code have withstood judicial scrutiny and are not violations of the ADEA. Thus, it may be permissible (depending on your state law) for a police department to inquire about the age of an applicant requesting to take a civil service exam. However, once it is determined that the applicant satisfies the necessary age requirements, further consideration of the applicant's age is improper and should be avoided.

Specific Prohibitions of the ADEA

- Governs employers with twenty (20) or more employees. This would be all the employees of a city, township, or county.
- The ADEA applies to state and political subdivisions, as well as the federal government. Therefore, it is illegal for city police departments to discriminate against individuals on the basis of age.
- Specifically, the ADEA prohibits age discrimination in employment, discharge, promotion, or treatment of persons over the age of forty (40).
- The Department of Labor is vested with the power of authority to investigate all claims of age discrimination. Additionally, claims may be brought as private actions pursuant to Ohio law.
- Relief for violations of the ADEA include: reinstatement, injunctive and declaratory relief, and attorney's fees.

Because of the potential of liability for violations to the ADEA, employers should avoid discrimination based upon age at both the hiring interview and the tenure of employment.

Exceptions for Police

The ADEA provides for a specific, narrow exception to the ADEA for police officers. The ADEA provides:

It shall not be unlawful for an employer which is a State, a political subdivision of a State, an agency or instrumentality of a State or a political subdivision of a State, or an interstate agency to fail or refuse to hire or to discharge any individual because of such individual's age if such action is taken:

(1) with respect to the employment of an individual as a firefighter or law enforcement officer...
(2) pursuant to a bona fide hiring or retirement plan that is not a subterfuge to evade the purposes of this Act.

Therefore, age may be considered by the employer in certain, limited instances.

Additional justified considerations of age occur when:

- The employer's action must be pursuant to state or local law enacted prior to March 3, 1983 and for mandatory retirements occurring after the passage of this amendment. The mandatory age must be fifty-five (55) or the age established by the applicable state or local law, whichever is later.
- The ADEA defines law enforcement officers as those employees whose duties "are primarily the investigation, apprehension, or detention of individuals suspected or convicted of offense against criminals of a state." Therefore, the exception may not apply to all personnel of a police department.
- The employer must have a good faith belief that the mandatory retirement age serves a legitimate police enforcement purpose.

Absent any of the above justifications for an action by an employer based upon age, the employer must not consider age.

Other Affirmative Defenses

Although it is illegal to discriminate against an individual on the basis of age, the ADEA does provide for five (5) affirmative defenses that apply to all employers. The defenses are:

- Age is a bona fide occupational qualification reasonably necessary to the normal operations of the particular business;
- The action is based upon reasonable factors other than age;
- The action was based upon a bona fide seniority system;
- The action was made in effort to observe the terms of a bona fide employee benefit plan;
- The discharge or other discipline of the individual was for cause.

As indicated above, it may be permissible for example for a government agency to require that all applicants be between the ages of twenty-one (21) and thirty-five (35) to be hired based on an established retirement system. However, after the initial age requirement is satisfied, the employer should ask no further questions regarding an applicant's age, or make further employment decisions based upon age, unless the above affirmative defenses are satisfied.

Title VII

Title VI of the Civil Rights Act of 1964 (Title VII) prohibits employment discrimination based on race, color, sex, religion, or national origin. In addition to protecting individuals from intentional discrimination on the basis of race, color, religion, sex, or national origin, Title VII also protects individuals from acts that have a discriminating effect based upon the aforementioned characteristics.

Title VII governs all state and local governments employing fifteen (15) or more individuals.

Prohibited Discriminatory Practices

Title VII prohibits the following discriminatory acts.

- Harassment of an individual on the basis of their race, color, religion, sex, or national origin.

- Retaliation against an individual for filing a charge of discrimination.
- Participating in an investigation, or openly opposing the discriminatory practices of an employer.
- Basing employment decisions on stereotypes or assumptions about the abilities, traits, or performance of individuals of a certain sex, race, age, religion, or ethnicity.
- Denying employment opportunities to a person because of marriage to, association with, an individual of a particular race, religion, sex, or national origin.

Because of the broad scope of Title VII, it is imperative that employers adhere to its prohibitions and guarantees. Therefore, employers must avoid interview questions or other pre-employment inquiries that may be construed to result in discriminatory acts that violate Title VII.

Employers guilty of intentionally discriminating against an employee in violation of Title VII are subject to both compensatory and punitive damages, attorney's fees, and the possibility of jury trials.

National Origin Discrimination

Title VII prohibits the discrimination of an individual on the basis of their birthplace, ancestry, culture, or linguistic characteristics that are common to a specific ethnic group.

Although questions regarding an individual's national origins should be avoided, the Immigration Reform and Control Act (IRCA) of 1986 requires that employers assure that hired employees are authorized to work in the United States. Therefore, employers must ascertain whether all of its employees are permitted to work in the U.S.

Caution: Employers must ask all employees of their ability to work in the U.S. Solely requesting verification of individuals of a particular origin or individuals who appear or sound foreign is likely a violation of Title VII. Thus, the safest employment practice is to inquire of all employees of their ability to work in the United States and require proof of the ability to work on the application.

Religious Discrimination

An employer cannot refuse to hire, discipline, discharge, or otherwise discriminate against an applicant or an employee on the basis of the individual's religion. Further, an employer may be required to reasonably accommodate the religious beliefs of an employee or prospective employee should it be necessary. However, any accommodation is unnecessary if it would pose an undue hardship on the employer.

Sex Discrimination

The sex discrimination prohibitions in Title VII are quite broad. For example, employers cannot engage in practices consisting of requests for sexual favors in exchange of favorable working conditions for persons of either gender or refuse to hire an individual on the basis of sex. However, employment decisions can be based on an individual's gender, if gender is a legitimate BFOQ. For example, being female may be a legitimate BFOQ for working in a jail with female inmates.

Title VII also prohibits the discrimination of an employee based on an applicant's pregnancy. Pregnancy, childbirth, or other related conditions must be treated the same as other temporary conditions or illnesses. Thus, no discussion of the applicant's desire to have a family or children should be discussed. Even casual inquiries that are innocent in nature could be the basis of a lawsuit.

All inquiries of job applicants should be job related. Therefore, questions should pertain to successful job performance without regard to an applicant's race, sex, national origin, or religious affiliation. Employers must be able to justify all requirements and inquiries as job related.

Employers must avoid all inquiries — even innocent inquiries — into a prospective employee's race, national origin, or religion as rejected applicants have a long memory and may use the employer's innocent queries as a basis for a lawsuit. Title VII provides a broad scope of claims for employees alleging discrimination.

References

Undoubtedly, the face-to-face interview and application process is one of the most integral and important features of the hiring process. Although much information concerning an applicant can be obtained by employers directly from the applicant, it is necessary and recommended that all employers perform reference checks on all candidates for employment. By checking references, employers will learn of any problems that the applicant had during prior employment.

The performance of reference checks, however, is not without its legal hazards. Again, the laws pertaining to information obtained during the course of performing reference checks highlights the balance that must be struck between the employer's need to gather information and the employee's right to keep personal information private. To the degree that an employer seeks information beyond the scope of what an employee is willing to share, privacy interests can be implicated. The following is a guide to examining and providing references.

As with questions regarding all pre-employment inquiries, questions in reference checks should be phrased so as to avoid violating state and federal law. Employers must remember that certain questions may result in responses regarding age, sex, national origin, a disability, religion and/or race.

Remember, because of potential lawsuits against them, prior employers are many times reluctant to provide opinions. Always ask for information that is or can be documented for your protection and for the protection of the previous employer. Consider reviewing or requesting copies of the applicant's job description and contents of their personnel file which is public record (non-personal information).

Questions Employers Cannot Ask:

- Did she seem interested in having children?
- Was she married when you knew her?
- Did she go to church on Sundays?
- Do you know where she was born?
- Did she belong to any clubs or organizations and could you give me all their names?
- Any question about the applicant's disability, illness, or workers' compensation history.

Employers Can Ask:

- Was he/she responsible?
- Was he/she prompt?
- Did he/she get along with other employees?
- What were her duties?
- Was his/her attendance record satisfactory?
- How did he/she perform her duties?
- Did he/she receive any promotions or job transfers?

Providing a Reference

In addition to legal concerns associated with seeking a reference, employers must also be concerned not to provide any unlawful information when providing a reference.

In the area of law enforcement, it is illegal to provide certain information. Therefore, it is necessary to always ensure compliance with your state public records laws. As an aside, prior to complying with any public records request, it is imperative to review the information that can and cannot be distributed to the public and how those restrictions apply to any request for public documents.

Additionally, employers must be concerned with the potential consequences of providing a negative reference. Because a negative reference can damage a former employee's job prospects and give rise to claims for defamation and invasion of privacy, an employer should proceed cautiously in providing any information beyond the name, position occupied, and dates of employment.

In answering questions concerning a former employee, the employer should adhere to the following suggestions.

- Be careful not to make technically accurate but misleading statements, i.e., "he was terminated for drug use," but fail to mention that he also accused his supervisor of racial prejudice.
- Be cautious in revealing any information, even when trying to be honest and helpful to a prospective employer, that might bring about an action for discrimination, e.g. the applicant "was difficult to get along with; he seemed very defensive about having been born in Iraq." The former

employee may bring an action against you alleging a claim of national origin discrimination pursuant to Title VII.

Be honest in your factual statement without being malicious. Always think through the implications of your comments: Does this information reveal anything about the former employee's race, sex, religion, age, national origin, etc.?

Employers must always remember that they are granted a qualified privilege for providing information during a reference check. As a result, employers will likely be found free from liability for any statements made during the process of providing a reference, so long as there is a truth in the statements made, and the statements are consistent with documentation of the employer.

Permissible and Impermissible Pre-Employment Inquiries

As noted above, because of the potential of liability for employers discriminating against a person on the basis of race, color, sex, religion, national origin, age, and disability, it is vital that employers obtain information of an applicant without violating that applicant's rights.

All government agencies should obtain legal advice on the appropriate and inappropriate manner to obtain necessary and relevant information.

Conclusion: General Interviewing

Principles

- Make sure all pre-employment inquiries are job related. All candidates should be considered solely on the basis of their qualifications and the likelihood of successful job performance. At no point during the pre-employment process should the candidate's race, gender, sex, disability, or any other unlawful criteria be considered (unless for legitimate BFOQ reasons).
- Avoid promises. Employers should not bind themselves to conditions regarding discharge, benefits and employee procedures and policies. The need to avoid promises regarding employment is especially true in the area of law enforcement

because of the presence of civil service rules and collective bargaining agreements. Any promise made in the hiring phases can be the basis of a contract or a promissory estoppel claim.

- Avoid subjective requirements and be prepared to justify all requirements as job related. The best defense to any lawsuit is that not only are the questions permissible but also that they are job related.
- Avoid casual, innocent inquiries into a candidate's race, national origin, religion, and gender. Innocent inquiries have-and will continue-to result in lawsuits and awards levied against employers.
- At the pre-employment stage, avoid asking a candidate about medical condition, diseases, hospitalization history, major illnesses, physical defects, disabilities, drug prescriptions, drug or alcohol addiction, or workers' compensation history. Such pre-employment inquiries are not proper pursuant to the ADA.
- Finally, employers must be aware of the potential liability for violations of an applicant or employee's civil rights. Discrimination lawsuits are costly. Remedies available for employment discrimination, whether intentional or unintentional, during both the pre-employment and employment phases, include:
  o Back pay,
  o Front-pay,
  o Hiring,
  o Any other action that will make Promotion the individual whole.
  o Reinstatement,
  o Attorneys' fees, Reasonable
  o Expert witness fees, and/or accommodation
  o Court costs.

Because of the potential liability, when in doubt, employers should not hesitate to consult the human resources staff or their attorneys. Ultimately, all established hiring policies and practices should be reviewed and approved by human resource staff and legal counsel.

Recommendations and Key Points for Legal Considerations for Entry Level Hiring

The following recommendations are made concerning legal considerations:

1. Candidates are garnered various legal protections by both state and federal law.
2. Employers must proceed cautiously, and be cognizant of questions and topics to avoid while conducting a thorough, productive and legal hiring process.
3. Employers must avoid asking illegal questions or seeking illegal information during the application process.
4. All legal issues, rules, and procedures apply to any outside firms obtained to assist in the hiring process.
5. The consideration of a law enforcement agency must be "how is the vacant position to be filled?" In other words, the vacancy must be filled pursuant to the law, civil service and any related bargaining agreement.
6. Civil service laws establish a merit system whereby selection or appointments and promotions may be made on the basis of demonstrated relative fitness and competence.
7. As a general rule, the employer should clearly indicate to the applicant the requirements of the position, as well as the procedures that will be utilized in filling the position.
8. Prior to a candidate taking an examination, reasonable notice of the exam must be given.
9. Courts have consistently ruled in favor of allowing a collective bargaining agreement to prevail over conflicting provisions in state or local laws, unless specifically exempted by law.
10. The Americans with Disability Act (ADA) prohibits discrimination against a qualified individual with a disability.
11. The essential functions of the job are the basic job duties that the individual must be able to perform with or without reasonable accommodation.
12. It is unlawful for an employer to discriminate against an employee on the basis of a disability. Employers must proceed with caution when interviewing applicants.

13. Title VI of the Civil Rights Act of 1964 (Title VII) prohibits employment discrimination based on race, color, sex, religion, or national origin
14. Make sure all pre-employment inquiries are job related. All candidates should be considered solely on the basis of their qualifications and the likelihood of successful job performance.
15. Ultimately, all established hiring policies and practices should be reviewed and approved by human resource staff and legal counsel.

Chapter 20

Using CALEA Standards for Recruitment and Selection

I had the honor and privilege to serve as a commissioner for the Commission on Accreditation for Law Enforcement Agencies (CALEA) for nine years. In my opinion these standards, which are developed and promulgated by law enforcement subject matter experts, are the critical benchmarks that should be used by all law enforcement agencies to manage in any of the topical areas they address. With permission from the CALEA, Chapter 31 on recruitment of law enforcement officers and Chapter 32 on the selection of law enforcement officers are reprinted here for law enforcement agencies to use to critique their current processes. A law enforcement agency that achieves compliance with these standards in the areas of recruitment and selection ensures that they are practicing the fundaments in these two areas of human resource management. It is, therefore, recommended that all law enforcement agencies work to achieve compliance in the areas of recruitment and selection with these standards. The four letters used after each accreditation standard indicate the levels of compliance based on agency size and denote the level of importance assigned to each standard.

The four agency size (number of personnel) categories are:

A. 1 – 24
B. 25 – 74
C. 75 – 289
D. 300 or more

Each of the four corresponding letters is sequenced from smallest to largest based on agency size.

STANDARDS FOR LAW ENFORCEMENT AGENCIES

The Standards Manual of
The Law Enforcement Agency
Accreditation Program

FIFTH EDITION REVISED
*Reprinted with permission from
the Commission on Accreditation for
Law Enforcement Agencies*

Commission on Accreditation
For Law Enforcement Agencies, Inc.

Chapters 31 & 32

CALEA Chapter 31

RECRUITMENT

A task as important as the recruitment and selection of law enforcement personnel should be approached from a positive viewpoint. Agencies, through the authority of their respective governments and administrations, should identify and employ the best candidates available, not merely eliminate the least qualified. The benefits of effective recruitment and selection policies are manifested in a lower rate of personnel turnover, fewer disciplinary problems, higher morale, better community relations, and more efficient and effective services.

The recruitment standards of the law enforcement accreditation process have embraced several important philosophical concepts in this chapter. The first concept is the expectation that an accredited agency will be an equal opportunity employer. Equal opportunity is the removal of barriers that prevent people from being treated fairly for employment purposes.

The second concept is the expectation that the agency's sworn work force will be representative of the available workforce in the agency's service community relative to its ethnic and gender composition. If any group is under-represented, the recruitment plan will include proactive steps to encourage members of that group to seek employment opportunities.

Under the International Law Enforcement accreditation program, the recruitment plan does not mandate hard quotas, such as hiring one female for every two males hired, nor is an agency expected to lower legitimate job-related hiring standards or criteria. Agencies are never expected to hire an individual who is not qualified to perform the duties of the job involved.

Agencies should be aware of several important assumptions that are built into the accreditation standards. Some standards are applicable only to those agencies with ongoing or active recruitment efforts. Agencies that only recruit to fill actual or forecast vacancies are relieved from continuous recruiting requirements but must comply with those standards that apply at the time of each recruiting campaign. However, two of the standards are operative for all agencies regardless of whether there are job vacancies: standard 31.2.1 establishing a recruitment plan if the proportion of minority group or women employees is lower than the proportion of these groups in the work force of the community, and standard 31.2.3 requiring an equal employment opportunity plan.

It is also understood that some agencies are required to handle their personnel through a state or local civil service merit system and are, therefore, linked to that system in the recruitment of law enforcement personnel. Obviously, every agency is obligated to comply with all applicable statutes and policy directives. However, the agency is required to show that the civil service agency upon which it depends is in compliance with applicable standards.

31.1   Administrative Practices and Procedures

31.1.1   Agency Participation

31.1.1   *The agency actively conducts, or participates in its recruitment program.*

Commentary: When the authority for recruitment is shared with other agencies, the law enforcement agency should seek to involve itself directly or indirectly in all activities critical to the recruitment effort. **(M M M M)**

31.1.2   Assignment/Recruitment

31.1.2 *Individuals assigned to recruitment activities are knowledgeable in personnel matters, especially equal employment opportunity.*

Commentary: Prior to initiating recruitment activities, recruiters should undergo a training program that provides knowledge and skills in the following areas: the agency's recruitment needs and commitments; agency career opportunities, salaries, benefits, and training; federal and state compliance guidelines; the community and its needs (including demographic data, community organizations, educational institutions, etc.); cultural awareness, or an understanding of different ethnic groups and subcultures; techniques of informal record-keeping systems for candidate tracking; the selection process utilized by the central personnel operation or agency (including procedures involved in conducting background investigations and written, oral, or physical agility examinations); recruitment programs of other jurisdictions; characteristics that disqualify candidates; and medical requirements. **(M M M M)**

31.2   Equal Employment Opportunity and Recruitment

31.2.1   Work Force Analysis

31.2.1 *The agency has ethnic and gender composition in the sworn law enforcement ranks in approximate proportion to the makeup of the available work force in the law enforcement agency's service community, or a recruitment plan pursuant to standard 31.2.2.*

Commentary: Recruitment steps should be directed towards the goal of approximating within the sworn ranks the demographic workforce composition of the community that it serves.

Statistics on the composition of the work force in the agency's service community are available from a variety of sources, such as the U.S. Department of Labor's Bureau of Labor Statistics or national labor statistics. For the purposes of this standard, available workforce may be determined by considering several factors; for example, the residential makeup, those working in the agency's community, applicant demographics, and the parameters of any officer residency requirements, if applicable. **(M M M M)**

31.2.2   Recruitment Plan

31.2.2 *The agency has a recruitment plan for full-time sworn personnel, that includes the following elements:*

 a. *statement of objectives;*
 b. *plan of action designed to achieve the objectives identified in bullet (a);*
 c. *procedures to evaluate the progress toward objectives every three years; and*
 d. *revise/reissue the plan as needed.*

Commentary: The recruitment plan should be written so that it can be easily understood and followed. The foundation of a successful recruitment drive should include strong management commitments, an analysis of demographic/geographic features of the agency's service area, and specific knowledge of past recruitment efforts by similar agencies. The recruitment plan may be a part of the written directive system or a separate and distinct planning document. The plan should govern agency activities relating to recruitment during a specific period of time, which should not exceed three years without being reviewed and having objectives updated.

The objectives of a recruitment plan should be reasonable, obtainable, and directed toward the goal of achieving a sworn work force that is representative of the composition of the available work force it serves. The specific action steps contained in the agency's recruitment plan should be reasonably likely to cause the agency to meet the objectives identified in the plan.

Examples of specific action steps that may be identified in an agency's recruitment plan include:

— utilizing in the agency's recruitment activities minority personnel who are fluent in the community's non-English languages and are aware of the cultural environment, where this would be applicable;
— depicting women and minorities in law enforcement employment roles in the agency's recruitment literature;
— conducting recruitment activities outside of the agency's jurisdiction, when necessary, to attract viable law enforcement candidates. Restricting recruiting to the agency's service area may limit the potential number of qualified applicants available from under-represented groups; and
— conducting periodically a "career" or "information" night for a particular target group. **(M M M M)**

31.2.3 Equal Employment Opportunity Plan (EEO)

31.2.3 *The agency has an equal employment opportunity plan.*

Commentary: The equal employment opportunity (EEO) plan should ensure equal opportunities for employment and employment conditions for minority persons and women. The equal employment opportunity plan should be based on an annual analysis of the agency's present employment policies, practices, and procedures relevant to their effective impact on the employment and utilization of minorities and women. The equal employment opportunity plan, which may be produced in the form of a written directive, may contain such provisions as: (1) a strongly worded statement from the agency's CEO that it is agency policy to ensure that all individuals be given equal opportunity for employment, regardless of race, sex, creed, color, age, religion, national origin, or physical impairment; (2) a procedure for filing complaints relating to EEO; and (3) specific action steps that the agency should take to ensure equal employment opportunity is a reality, such as advertising as an "equal opportunity employer" or providing applications or testing processes at decentralized, easily accessible locations. The policies relating to harassment in the workplace may also be incorporated into the agency's overall EEO effort (see standard 26.1.3). **(M M M M)**

31.3 Job Announcements and Publicity

31.3.1 Job Announcements

31.3.1 *The agency's job announcements and recruitment notices for all personnel:*
   a. *provide a description of the duties, responsibilities, requisite skills, educational level, and other minimum qualifications or requirements;*
   b. *advertise entry-level job vacancies through electronic, print, or other media;*
   c. *advertise the agency as an equal opportunity employer on all employment applications and recruitment advertisements; and*
   d. *advertise official application filing deadlines.*

Commentary: The agency should provide the most accurate and precise job description possible to avoid undue delay and wasted time on the part of the agency and the applicant. When the most important performance dimensions are known, potential applicants are in a better position to relate their particular knowledge, understanding, and skills to those required by the position to be filled. The agency saves the time and expense of making determinations that the applicants could have made, had they been fully apprised.

The agency should ensure that job announcements do not set standards or criteria that even unintentionally screen out, or tend to screen out, an individual with a disability or class of individuals with disabilities, unless the criteria are job-related and consistent with business necessity. Job announcements should not set standards that cannot be specifically supported and should avoid general requirements such as "excellent health" or "no history of psychological or emotional disorders." (Refer to Section 102, Americans with Disabilities Act.) **(M M M M)**

31.3.2 Posting Locations

31.3.2 *The agency posts all job announcements with community service organizations and/or seeks cooperative assistance from community organization key leaders.*

Commentary: The agency should seek permission to post job announcements with community organizations that are in contact with individuals who are likely candidates for recruitment. The agency should seek to achieve broader dissemination and greater exposure of recruitment information. The agency should consider technological resources, such as the Internet, when posting all job announcements.
(O M M M)

31.3.3   Maintaining Applicant Contact

31.3.3   *Contact is maintained with applicants for all positions from initial application to final employment disposition.*

Commentary: Applicants should be periodically informed of the status of their applications. Applicant contacts should be documented and logged. The agency should consider technological resources for maintaining contact with applicants. **(M M M M)**

31.3.4   Application Rejection

31.3.4   *Applications for all positions are not rejected because of minor omissions or deficiencies that can be corrected prior to the testing or interview process.*

Commentary: Applications that are deficient should be processed routinely if the deficiency can be rectified prior to the testing or interview process. **(M M M M)**

CALEA Chapter 32

SELECTION

The selection process is defined as the combined effect of components and procedures leading to the final employment decision. It is a key component in defining the operational effectiveness of a law enforcement agency. All jurisdictions necessarily differ in a variety of unique and important ways regarding personnel selection. Nevertheless, basic principles exist for the development of an efficient, effective, and fair selection process that results in the appointment of those individuals who best possess the skills, knowledge, and abilities (SKA) necessary for an effective, respected law enforcement agency.

A job-related, useful, and nondiscriminatory selection process is dependent upon a number of professionally and legally accepted administrative practices and procedures, which include informing candidates of all parts of the selection process at the time of formal application; maintaining written procedures governing lateral entry and reapplication of unsuccessful candidates; and ensuring timely notification of candidates about their status at all critical points in the process. These procedures and practices significantly contribute to a more efficient, effective, and fair selection process.

It is understood that some agencies are required to handle their personnel through a state or local civil service merit system and are, therefore, linked to that system in the selection of their law enforcement personnel. Every agency is obligated to comply with all applicable statutes and policy directives. This may result in the agency being unable to unilaterally comply with certain standards, but Guiding Principle 1.2 requires the agency to seek compliance from outside sources. The agency is required to show that the civil service agency upon which it depends is in compliance with applicable standards.

32.1   Professional and Legal Requirements

32.1.1 Selection Process Described

32.1.1 *Written directives describe all elements and activities of the selection process for all full-time personnel.*

Commentary: Such written directives are essential for the proper administration, use, and defensibility of the selection process. The directive should describe the order of events in the selection process and should include, at the least, information about the purpose, development, job relatedness, administration, scoring, and interpretation of all elements used in the selection process. The law enforcement agency may rely upon a state or local civil service commission, employment agency, or other public or private organization to administer or provide one or more elements of the selection process. If so, a copy of all relevant manuals should be maintained on file by the law enforcement agency. Written directives should describe the selection process in detail and include timetables, the order of events, administration, scoring, interpretation of test results, and other pertinent information. **(M M M M)**

32.1.2 Job Relatedness

32.1.2 *All elements of the selection process for sworn personnel use only those rating criteria or minimum qualifications that are job related.*

Commentary: The intent of this standard is to ensure that candidates are evaluated by a selection process that measures traits or characteristics that are a significant part of the job. It is not sufficient for an agency to merely say in a directive that its procedures are job related.

There are a variety of means by which job-relatedness can be shown. An agency may choose, for example, to demonstrate that an oral examination measures traits that are shown by the task analysis to be significant or necessary to perform the job. An assessment center may be shown to measure the performance of tasks or skills that the task description has shown to be essential job functions (see Chapter 21 regarding task analysis and job descriptions).

The agency may also demonstrate job-relatedness through a process which validates the selection mechanism as a predictor of future job success. A written test may be statistically validated as being able to assess skills necessary for the job of sworn officer. Many commercially produced tests have documentation that will support validation. Agencies are encouraged to seek assistance in this area from competent personnel resources as many of the validation concepts are technical and/or unfamiliar to police professionals.

Nothing in this standard should be interpreted as preventing an agency from using a combination of methods to document the job-relatedness of its selection process. The goal of this standard is to ensure that the agency has the documentation necessary to make a logical and persuasive case, in the event of a legal challenge, that the elements of the selection process measure skills, knowledge, abilities, and traits needed to perform that job. **(M M M M)**

32.1.3   Uniform Administration

32.1.3   *A written directive requires that all elements of the selection process for all personnel be administered, scored, evaluated, and interpreted in a uniform manner within the classification.*

Commentary: Operational elements of the selection process-time limits, oral instructions, practice problems, answer sheets, and scoring formulas-should be clearly set forth and carried out identically for all candidates. Failure to do so may preclude validation of the process and make the agency susceptible to legal challenges. **(M M M M)**

32.1.4   Candidate Information

32.1.4   *At the time of their formal application, candidates for all positions are informed, in writing, of:*
   a.   all elements of the selection process;
   b.   the expected duration of the selection process; and
   c.   the agency's policy on reapplication.

Commentary: A listing of selection elements should include, but is not limited to, all written physical and psychological examinations, polygraph examinations, oral interviews, and background investigations. From the outset, candidates should be made aware that sensitive or confidential aspects of their personal lives may be explored. Written notification of the expected duration of the selection process not only is a courtesy but also helps the agency better plan and coordinate its selection process. **(M M M M)**

32.1.5   Notification of Ineligibility

32.1.5   *All candidates not selected for positions are informed in writing.*

Commentary: Prompt notification in writing is not only an essential element of an efficient administrative organization but also is fundamental to a fair and effective selection process. Candidates should be informed within 30 days of such a decision. **(M M M M)**

32.1.6   Records

32.1.6   *A written directive governs the disposition of the records of all candidates not selected for appointment.*

Commentary: It is necessary to maintain selection data to ensure continuing research, independent evaluation, and defense against lawsuits. The agency should determine requirements, consistent with applicable laws, for maintaining identifying information, such as names and addresses. The agency should comply with all federal, state, and local requirements regarding the privacy, security, and freedom of information of all candidate records and data. **(M M M M)**

32.1.7   Selection Material Security

32.1.7   *A written directive requires that selection materials be stored in a secure area when not being used and are disposed of in a manner that prevents disclosure of the information within.*

Commentary: The agency responsible for selection materials should limit access to them and store them in locked files to provide 24-hour security. Selection materials should not be left unattended. **(M M M M)**

32.2   Administrative Practices and Procedures

32.2.1   Background Investigations

32.2.1 *A background investigation of each candidate for all positions is conducted prior to appointment to probationary status, and includes:*
a. *verification of qualifying credentials;*
b. *a review of any criminal record; and*
c. *verification of at least three personal references.*

Commentary: It is more reliable to conduct the inquiry in person, though telephone and mail inquiries are appropriate in obtaining criminal history and driving records. The investigation should routinely involve a home visit with the candidate and his or her family and interviews with neighbors. Background investigations are generally listed among the final stages in the selection process only to suggest that this is when they should be completed; they are likely to have commenced much earlier. **(M M M M)**

32.2.2   Training

32.2.2 *Personnel used to conduct background investigations are trained in collecting required information.*

Commentary: None. **(M M M M)**

32.2.3   Records Retention

32.2.3 *The agency has a policy regarding the retention of each candidate's background information.*

Commentary: None. **(M M M M)**

Change Notice 5.8 (March 26, 2010)

32.2.4   Polygraph Examinations

32.2.4 *If polygraph examinations or other instruments for the detection of deception are used in the selection process, candidates are provided with a list of areas from which polygraph questions will be drawn, prior to such examination.*

Commentary: Agencies are not required to administer polygraph examinations or other truth verification tests to all job classifications. For example, polygraph examinations may be required for sworn personnel but need not be required for non-sworn personnel. **(M M M M)**

32.2.5   Conducted by Trained Personnel

32.2.5   *If polygraph examinations or other instruments for the detection of deception are used in the selection process, the administration of examinations and the evaluation of results are conducted by personnel trained in these procedures.*

Commentary: The sensitive nature of these tests makes it necessary to rely upon examiners who possess professional training and credentials in the use and interpretation of these investigative tools. **(M M M M)**

32.2.6   Use of Results

32.2.6   *A written directive prohibits the use of results of polygraph examinations or other instruments for the detection of deception as the single determinant of employment status.*

Commentary: Authorities agree that polygraph examinations or other instruments for the detection of deception should be used only as an investigative aid, if at all. An admission during pre-test, test, or post-test interviews, together with other information, may be sufficient to support decisions relevant to employment status. **(M M M M)**

32.2.7   Medical Examinations

32.2.7   *A medical examination is conducted, prior to appointment to probationary status, to certify the general health of each candidate for a sworn position.*

Commentary: None. **(M M M M)**

32.2.8   Emotional Stability/Psychological Fitness Examinations

32.2.8   *An emotional stability and psychological fitness examination of each candidate for a sworn position is conducted and assessed by a qualified professional prior to appointment to probationary status.*

Commentary: None. **(M M M M)**

32.2.9   Records Retention

32.2.9   *The agency has a policy regarding the retention of the results of medical examinations, emotional stability and psychological fitness examinations.*

Commentary: The agency should maintain a report of each physical examination and emotional stability and psychological fitness examination to ensure proper procedures are followed and to provide data for continuing research and legal defense, if needed. All records should be stored in a secure area. Access should be restricted to those persons legally entitled to review these records. The files or records may be maintained in agency files or at the location of the medical examination provider. **(M M M M)**

Change Notice 5.8 (March 26, 2010)

32.2.10   Entry Level Probation

32.2.10   *In the absence of controlling legislation, or a collective bargaining agreement, at least a six-month probationary period for sworn personnel following completion of entry-level classroom training is required before candidates are granted permanent status.*

Commentary: The agency should include a probationary period among the final steps in the selection process. A six-month probationary period is generally accepted as a minimum among the law enforcement community and should be carefully related to the field training program (see standard 33.4.3). Exceptions to the probation period if any, should be described in the directive. Exceptions may include special assignments, injury, or illness occurring during entry-level training and remedial training. **(M M M M)**

Change Notice 5.8 (March 26, 2010)

Transformational Leadership

To raise retention rates in law enforcement, an agency must focus on the quality of its leadership. The decision to stay or leave a law enforcement agency is often based on the effectiveness of the police leadership team or one's relationship with their individual manager. The benefit of improving the recruitment and selection practices cannot be fully realized unless an agency is able to retain those officers after they are hired. Therefore, the quality of police leadership will have a direct impact on the retention of an agency's law enforcement officers. A leadership style that has been researched and recommended as effective for law enforcement executives is "transformational leadership." This style of leadership not only helps to facilitate the transformation of the organization, but it also transforms its people.

How does a police chief go beyond accomplishing the mission and goals of an organization to effecting organizational change in a personal and compelling way to motivate people? In pursuit of this question, leadership researchers recently directed their attention to those remarkable leaders who inspire superlative performance. The phenomenon they found is called, "Transformational Leadership Theory." A transformational leadership style is highly beneficial for police chiefs as the following leadership material will explain.

To understand the benefits of transformational leader to the police chief, it is helpful to contrast it with traditional or transactional leadership. The traditional or transactional police chief as a leader uses a cost-benefit or quid pro quo approach to motivating followers. This leader provides what a group needs in exchange for their performance. The transactional leader is responsive to his or her followers immediate self-interest and needs, leading by exchanging pay, status, promotion, and similar rewards for work effort. Transactional leadership relies on equity and reciprocity to achieve compliance.

The transformational leader, on the other hand, elicits more than mere compliance from followers. This concept of leadership envisions a transformation of followers' values and attitudes, thus motivating them to perform. Such a leader goes beyond basic emotions such as fear, jealousy, or greed. The leader appeals to ideals and moral values such as justice, patriotism, or self-improvement. Transformational leaders motivate their followers to forsake self-interest for the advancement of group or organizational goals. They ask followers to transcend personal needs and, yet, still accomplish them through the achievement of team, unit, or organizational goals. Follower performance stems from the internalization of values rather than the appeal of rewards, threats of punishment, or gratification of other personal needs. A transformational leader actively seeks the achievement of new attitudes, motivation, and behaviors from their followers.

It is important to note that the transactional and transformational leadership styles can co-exist comfortably. These two styles of leadership are not mutually exclusive. In fact, every transformational leader should first become a competent, effective transactional manager. The use of reward power, coercive power, equity, and expectancy all have a necessary place in the transformational leader's approach.

The transformational leadership style is one in which there is shared leadership and shared vision, which result in the continuing improvement of the individual. This is a dynamic social process resulting from interaction between the leader and followers. In an article written for *Police Chief Magazine* titled, "Transformational Leadership and Staff Training in the Law Enforcement Profession," author Bay Bynum discusses "four I's" of leadership that help formulate a leader's transformational leadership style.

The first "I" is, "Individualized consideration" of the person being lead, which means the leader must take into account the differences of their followers.

The second "I" is, "Idealized influence," which influence allows for potential transformation.

The third "I" is "Inspirational motivation," which indicates the leader is facilitating the follower's desire to achieve organizational goals.

The fourth "I" is "Intellectual stimulation," which is indicative of the educational component of a transformational leadership style. The use of these components causes the leader to treat followers as individuals and not members of a group.

The leader's support, encouragement, and motivation enable individuals to perform at a much higher level (Bynum, 2008).

What do law enforcement officers think about the effectiveness of police leadership? An article from *Police Chief Magazine* titled, "Preparing Leaders for Law Enforcement," by authors Morreale and Ortmeier provide some insight into this question. In a study conducted by Morreale indicated that line officers reported increased job satisfaction and exerted extra effort when their leaders demonstrated transformational leadership. These transformational leaders are individuals who set high standards of conduct, become role models, gain the trust of their subordinates, get the respect and confidence of others, articulate the future desired state and plan to achieve it, question the status quo, and continuously innovate (Morreale & Ortmeier, 2004). All of these characteristics and abilities focus on interpersonal leader behaviors. These authors clearly and correctly describe a key element of police executive leadership as decision making. The decisions made by police leaders are distinct from those made by their officers instantly in the field. In most situations there is time to reflect, assess, and collect data to make informed decisions. The development of a systematic decision-making process is beneficial to the degree it includes collecting and evaluating information and data, giving other stakeholders the opportunity to review it, consider policing best practices, and provide input for organizational decision making. Although it is easy to maintain the status quo, the challenge is to identify and encourage staff to support and keep pace with the need for change. Most government organizations are bureaucratic and do not facilitate or encourage the creativity and innovation necessary to accommodate change (Morreale & Ortmeier, 2004).

In another article from *Police Chief Magazine* titled, "The changing Face of Police Leadership" authors Todd Wuestewald and Brigitte Steinheider state, "If our ideas about leadership in the past tended to revolve around the solitary heroic figure, the leadership of our future will be defined by inspired teamwork." They clarify this statement by indicating that the style and practice of police leadership are gradually evolving. The trend is turning to the multi-faceted nature of teamwork, inclusion, and diverse leadership. It is a view that leadership is broadly distributed among coworkers rather than being concentrated in the hands of one or a few superiors (Wuestewald & Steinheider, 2006).

The information contained in the various articles provides a description of the value and relevance of a transformational leadership style for a police chief. Transformational leadership recognizes that the role of the police chief is to institutionalize positive change for both the individual and the organization consistent with its mission and goals.

A core message to the management of law enforcement agencies is practice participative management. When is it appropriate, involve the people who have a stake in the outcome of the decisions in the decision-making process. The principle in play is, if there is no involvement at some level, then there is no commitment to the outcome.

Personnel Decisions

I have previously indicated that the most important decision a manager can make is a hiring decision. I believe the next two important decisions are where to assign individuals and who to promote. Therefore, law enforcement managers (or any other organizational manager) can conclude that the most significant decisions are the personnel decisions. It is the people you hire, where you assign them, and who you promote that will determine the effectiveness of a law enforcement agency. Jim Collins, in his best-selling book titled *Good to Great*, indicates the value and importance of effective personnel decisions. This book describes 11 companies that made the transition from being a good company to a great company and how they did it. Chapter 3 of this book titled, "First Who ... Then What," articulates that effective personnel selection is one of the key components of an organization transitioning from being good to becoming great. In this chapter, Jim Collins uses the metaphor of the bus in relation to personnel selection. He indicates that managers must first get the right people on the bus, "hire the right people." Second, they must get the "right people in the right seats" (meaning their assignment should be in alignment with their skill set and abilities). Third, they should get the "wrong people off the bus" (meaning firing those people who are either ineffective in their job or not compatible with the organization's goals, mission, and values). Nucor, one of the 11 companies that made the good to great transformation, rejected the old adage that people are your most important asset. They believe that people are not the most important asset, but the right people are. In alignment with this comment, a Wells Fargo executive stated, "The only way to deliver to the people who are achieving is to not burden them with the people who are not achieving" (Collins, 2001).

Nucor also reinforces a key point made throughout this book: in selecting "the right people," the good-to-great companies place greater weight on character attributes than on specific educational background, practical skills, specialized work-related knowledge, or work experience. The company did not view specific knowledge or skills as unimportant, but they viewed these traits as both more teachable and learnable. They believe that behavioral dimensions like character, work ethic, and values are more ingrained.

Organizational Statements

One of the primary responsibilities of a law enforcement chief executive officer is to establish organizational statements for the law enforcement agency. There are four significant types of organizational statements: Vision, Mission, Major Goals, and Core Values. Police leadership enhances law enforcement retention by clearly articulating these four organizational elements. Individuals are recruited by and drawn to the organization because their skill set, interest, personality, and values are compatible with that of a law enforcement agency. When a law enforcement agency has established organizational statements, individual compatibility can be assessed.

A Vision statement describes what an organization wants to become three to five years in the future. The chief executive officer of an organization is responsible for facilitating the development of this futuristic statement that spawns excitement. The Mission of an organization flows out of the Vision.

A Mission statement describes who an organization is, what it does, who it does it for, and how it does it differently from others in their same line of work. Mission statements need to be revised every three to five years. A Mission statement is foundational because it describes the organization's purpose.

The Major Goals of the organization are the practical steps necessary in the achievement of the organization's Mission. For Goals to be valuable, they must be specific and measurable, while accomplished within a specified period of time. The establishment of Goals flows out of the Mission.

A law enforcement agency's Core Values are the conduct and character exhibited by every member of the organization while they are achieving the Mission. Law enforcement Core Values are to be modeled on or off duty by its officers. The rules and regulations of a law enforcement agency reinforce its Core Values. Core Values guide how all employees treat members of the community and one another.

The Appendix in this chapter contains a description of organizational statements and the key elements of each type of organizational statement.

Every law enforcement agency should require that essential signatory documents be signed by its law enforcement officer candidates as a condition of employment. This is to ensure that they are compatible with both the professional and organizational philosophies and policies. The first step in keeping officers is ensuring they are the right organizational fit. The following is a list of recommended signatory documents that should be utilized by every law enforcement agency:

1. Organizational statements, which consist of Core Values, Vision Statement, and Mission Statement;
2. The Law Enforcement Code of Ethics;
3. Canons of Law Enforcement Ethics; and
4. The Law Enforcement Oath of Honor.

The agency should establish a Recruitment and Retention Advisory Council whose members represent a cross section of private and public employees, community members, and stake-holders of those receiving law enforcement services.

Key stakeholders, subject matter experts, private and public organizations can yield a wealth of information concerning effective practices in the recruitment and retention of law enforcement officers. These individuals or groups are also a good source for marketing and sharing information regarding recruitment. The Recruitment Advisory Council should be a diverse group of community members based on age, gender, ethnicity, residents of the community, business owners, organizational employees, school district representatives, and elected officials.

Recommendations and Key Points of Management Issues in the Retention of Officers

1. Transformational leadership is effective because it transforms a follower's values and attitudes, thus motivating them to perform.
2. It is important to note that the transactional and transformational leadership styles can co-exist comfortably.
3. There are four I's of leadership that help formulate a leader's transformational leadership style. They are individualized consideration, idealized influence, inspirational motivation, and intellectual stimulation.
4. In transformational leadership, the leader's support, encouragement, and motivation enable individuals to perform at a much higher level.
5. Most government organizations are bureaucratic and do not facilitate or encourage the creativity and innovation necessary to accommodate change.
6. The trend in law enforcement is turning to the multifaceted nature of teamwork, inclusion, and diverse leadership.
7. Law enforcement managers (or any other organizational manager) should know that the most significant decisions are the personnel decisions. It is the people you hire, where you assign them, and whom you promote that will determine the effectiveness of a law enforcement agency.
8. People are not the most important asset, but the right people are.
9. The only way to deliver to the people who are achieving is to not burden them with the people who are not achieving.
10. Hiring individuals based on behavioral dimensions like character, work ethic, and values are more effective than hiring for specific job knowledge or skills.

11. The retention of law enforcement officers is enhanced when police leadership clearly articulates the Vision, Mission, Major Goals, and Core Values of the organization.
12. When a law enforcement agency has established organizational statements, individual compatibility can be assessed.
13. Every law enforcement agency should require that essential signatory documents be signed by its law enforcement officer candidates as a condition of employment.
14. The agency should establish a Recruitment and Retention Advisory Council whose members represent a cross section of private and public employees, community members, and stakeholders of those receiving law enforcement services.

Appendix 21-1
Elements of Organizational Statements

VISION
A Vision Statement should answer the question, *"What do we want this organization to be like three to five years from now?"* A Vision Statement should include the following principle elements . . .

1. Be clear
2. Be expressed in present tense
3. Use visionary terms to spawn excitement

MISSION
A Mission Statement for an organization should clearly address the question, *"What are our organization's primary assignments in striving toward our vision?"* The Mission Statement should meet, at a minimum, the following principle elements . . .

1. Who we are
2. What we do
3. Who we do it for
4. How we do it

CORE VALUES
Core Values are the conduct and character exhibited by every member of the organization while achieving the Mission. Core Values describe . . .

1. Character
2. Conduct
3. Behaviors

GOALS
Goals should specifically answer the question, *"What do we have to do to accomplish our Mission while striving toward our Vision?"* To do this, Goals should meet the following principle elements . . .

1. S.M.A.R.T.
2. Specific
3. Measurable

4. Attainable
5. Realistic
6. Time-based

References

Bynum, R. (February 2008). *Transformational leadership and staff training in the law enforcement profession. Police Chief Magazine.*

Collins, J. (2001). *Good to great.* New York, NY: Harper Collins Publishers Inc.

Morreale, S. A., & Ortmeier, P.J. (October 2004). *Preparing leaders for law enforcement. Police Chief Magazine.*

Wuestewald, T., & Steinheider, B. (April 2006). *The Changing Face of Police Leadership. Police Chief Magazine.*

Chapter 22

Mentoring Law Enforcement Officers

Mentoring: Its Importance and Value

To effectively fill future law enforcement positions with qualified and competent officers, certain training and qualification standards must precede one's selection for the job. Once a person is assigned to an entry-level officer position, he/she must be ready and prepared to function effectively as a law enforcement officer. In addition to training, a mentoring program may assist in preparing officers to become competent in the job. Additionally, officers can be prepared to fill the management role left void by a superior officer. A mentor, as defined by the Merriam-Webster dictionary, is "a trusted counselor or guide" (Mentor). A mentor typically is a senior, experienced employee who serves as a role model, provides support, direction, and feedback to the younger employee regarding career plans, and interpersonal development, to guide and influence career opportunities. Mentoring can be found in a variety of forms, but always involves a relationship between an experienced mentor and an inexperienced mentee who wishes to learn from the mentor's experience.

This topic is vital because it significantly impacts the structure and stability of a law enforcement agency. The idea of a mentor as one with experience teaches, advises, and shares wisdom with one who hopes to hold the same or similar position as the more experienced individual. The more experienced and skilled person is known as the mentor while the less-skilled and inexperienced individual is known as a mentee or a protégé (Sprafka & Kranda, 2008, p. 47). Mentoring not only concerns the future of leadership of a law enforcement agency, but it concerns the interagency relationships as well as the agency's relationship with its community.

The idea of a mentor-mentee relationship is not a new or revolutionary idea. On the contrary, the idea of a mentor, in its modern definition, was first referenced in 1699 by a French novelist, Francois Fenelon (Roberts, 1999, p. 313). The term mentor is derived from of a Greek mythological character that formed a father-like relationship with the son of Odysseus. During the Middle Ages, this concept was often seen in an apprentice relationship in which a boy or young man would live with and assist masters in craft or trade. During his years of assistance, the young man gains experience and eventually becomes a master in that particular trade. This apprenticeship concept was also very common during the American Colonial period. Young apprentices would spend an average of seven years with their masters as they assisted him and learned the craft or trade.

In the field of law enforcement, the mentor is the ranking officer and the mentee is the subordinate officer who desires to hold a ranking or higher position.

The Structure, Purpose, and Design of a Mentoring Program

Mentoring programs can be initiated either by an individual looking for advice or required by the agency that employs the individual. Mentoring sessions may occur face-to-face, telephonically, or through email communication. Face-to-face sessions may take place in formal settings such as an office or in informal settings such as a restaurant. Mentoring programs can be very rigid with bi-weekly meetings or loosely organized with bi-monthly sessions. Mentoring sessions can be organized as lectures, conversations, question and answer sessions, or alternative learning methods. While the style or function of the mentoring program may vary, a common set of goals perseveres. These goals are to promote professional growth, inspire personal motivation, and enhance effectiveness of police service (Sprafka & Kranda, 2008).

There are a series of key learning outcomes that a mentoring program strives to accomplish or achieve (there are benefits for both parties involved in the mentoring process). While the mentoring program is focused on preparing a mentee for a management position in law enforcement, there are benefits for the mentors, as well. According to the International Association of Chiefs of Police (IACP), the following outcomes are beneficial for the protégés in the mentoring program:

- Increases likelihood for success — mentors help protégés gain competency and avoid failure
- Assists protégés in setting goals and charting career paths

- Encourages and provides opportunities for new experiences and professional growth
- Helps the protégé avoid pitfalls and learn through real-life examples
- Enhances the protégé's feeling of worth to the mentor and the organization
- Encourages self-confidence by cheering protégé achievements

All of the above key outcomes are designed to assist the mentee in effectively transitioning to a position of leadership. As mentioned previously, the officer should first learn the entry-level job before beginning to transition into a management position. Mentoring subordinate officers is beneficial to their relationship with the department and the department's relationship with the community. If an officer can transition smoothly into a position of leadership, they will be able to more effectively take charge and presumably make fewer mistakes.

The protégé must have responsibilities during their time as a mentee if they are to effectively be impacted by the mentoring program. The following responsibilities are listed by the IACP (2006) in their comprehensive research of mentoring programs in police departments:

- Clearly defining personal employment goals
- Taking directions given and following through on them
- Accepting and appreciating mentoring assistance
- Listening to what others have to say
- Expressing appreciation
- Being assertive and asking good questions
- Asking for help when needed
- Sharing credit for a job well done with other team members
- Respecting mentors' time and agency responsibilities

The receptiveness and appreciativeness of the mentee is crucial to the effectiveness and impact of the mentoring program in his career. If one is to participate in a mentoring program, they must understand that it is a privilege to learn from those who have experience. Most mentoring programs are designed to assist those who will be in leadership and to prepare them to be better qualified for a management position.

Although the mentee has responsibilities and a set of clear, key learning outcomes, benefits exist for the mentor as well. A mentor may be volunteering his time and efforts to assist a protégé, and it must be remembered that benefits exist for them as well. In their study, the IACP (2008) identifies the following benefits for those who mentor in a mentoring program:

- A personal sense of reward for spotlighting and developing talent
- Enhanced knowledge of department policies and procedures as well as contemporary policing practices
- Paving the way for others, thereby leaving a positive legacy in the agency
- A reputation as a valuable member of the organization and the respect of colleagues
- Varying perspectives from protégés, which foster creativity
- "Getting by giving" in service to a subordinate professional

As benefits exist for mentors and mentees, responsibilities exist for both parties as well. Some departments incorporate a mentor program into an officer's work schedule and he will be compensated for his time and work with a mentee. In other departments, mentor programs take place outside normal work hours. This requires a superior and subordinate officer to volunteer their time to make such a program possible. The responsibilities of a mentor are listed by the IACP (2008) in a continuation of their study:

- Offering wise counsel
- Helping to build self-confidence
- Offering friendship and encouragement
- Providing information and resources
- Offering guidance, giving feedback, and cheering accomplishments
- Discussing and facilitating opportunities for new experiences and skill building
- Assisting in mapping a career plan

Both mentor and mentee play a crucial role in the effectiveness of a mentor program. Both parties must be willing to work together in attaining a common goal, which is to be of benefit to the agency the officers are employed by. The effectiveness of the protégé benefits the agency and the succession of leadership will be positively impacted if new leaders are formally mentored by their experienced superiors.

Needless to say, formal mentoring requires a conscious effort from both the mentor and the protégé. Both parties must want to learn from each other and support each other and have the desire to improve the quality of leadership at their department. A mentor-mentee relationship is not merely a professional or business relationship; rather, both parties must desire to build a personal relationship with each other. After some time, a formal mentoring relationship should begin to feel like an informal one as both parties begin to establish a friendship and a trust between them. The quality of the relationship is strongly related to the success of the mentoring program and, in many cases, the mentor and mentee work together in the future and do not simply end a relationship after the program is completed.

A mentoring program can supplement the field training officer's program. The program can be used to accelerate the learning process for the new officer. An effective mentoring program for new officers can improve both their job performance and job satisfaction. A mentoring program can reduce the time it takes to produce a fully functioning law enforcement officer.

The mentoring program may also seek to prevent a lack of preparation by those who serve in a management positions in law enforcement agencies. A mentoring program seeks to reduce the length of a transition time for a new ranking officer and reduce the number of mistakes that officer makes as he begins to transition. Essentially, a promotional development mentoring program seeks to increase the ease of promotion and give a recently promoted officer support to assist him or her in their transition into a management position.

Some Mentoring Strategies

If a law enforcement agency decides to develop and implement a mentoring program, some of the following guidelines are recommended.

- If the focus of a mentoring program is on the development of entry-level officers to become fully functioning in their job, then all officers should be mentored.
- Each officer should be assigned a mentor after completing the field training officer's program.
- A potential mentor should be provided a profile description to be matched with a protégé who shares similar interests and goals.
- A mentoring program to improve entry-level job effectiveness should last approximately two years.
- The mentor and mentee should meet weekly to discuss issues and answer questions.
- The protégé should use this as an opportunity to seek answers and advice from the mentor.
- The mentor may of course choose to discuss certain topics of interest or importance with the protégé. Ideally, the mentor and mentee will create a relationship that continues beyond a formal mentoring program.
- Same sex mentoring relationships only should be allowed to avoid any appearance or opportunity for sexual misconduct among coworkers.

If the focus of a law enforcement agency's mentoring program is the development of future managers, interested personnel are formally apply for the program. There should be an application process used to match mentors and mentees that are compatible. Ideally, the mentoring program should be installed for all ranking jobs with the exception of the police chief. A mentor should provide some assignments and tasks to be completed to help repair the mentee for future management position.

The mentoring of law enforcement officers is one of the most effective and practical ways to improve job performance or prepare officers for management position. Mentoring really is a highly effective succession planning process.

Recommendations and Key Points of Mentoring Law Enforcement Officers

1. A mentor is defined as a trusted counselor or guide.
2. A mentor typically is a senior, experienced employee who serves as a role model, provides support, direction, and feedback to the younger employee regarding career plans, and interpersonal development, to guide and influence career opportunities.
3. The idea of a mentor as one with experience teaches, advises, and shares wisdom with one who hopes to hold the same or similar position as the more experienced individual.
4. The more experienced and skilled person is known as the mentor while the less-skilled and inexperienced individual is known as the mentee or protégé.
5. Mentoring programs can be initiated either by an individual looking for advice or required by the agency that employs the individual.
6. Key outcomes of the mentoring program are designed to assist the mentee in effectively transitioning to a position of leadership.
7. The protégé must have responsibilities during their time as a mentee if they are to effectively be impacted by the mentoring program.
8. The receptiveness and appreciativeness of the mentee is crucial to the effectiveness and impact of the mentoring program in his career.
9. While the mentee has responsibilities and a set of clear, key learning outcomes, benefits exist for the mentor as well.
10. An effective mentoring program for new officers can improve both their job performance and job satisfaction.
11. A mentoring program for a new officer can reduce the time it takes to produce a fully functioning law enforcement officer.
12. Essentially, a promotional development mentoring program seeks to increase the ease of promotion and give a recently promoted officer support to assist him or her in their transition into a management position.
13. A mentoring program to improve entry-level job effectiveness should last approximately two years.

14. The mentor and mentee should meet weekly to discuss issues and answer questions.
15. Ideally, the mentor and mentee will create a relationship that continues beyond a formal mentoring program.
16. Same sex mentoring relationships only should be allowed to avoid any appearance or opportunity for sexual misconduct among coworkers.
17. The mentoring of law enforcement officers is one of the most effective and practical ways to improve job performance or prepare officers for management position.

References

Roberts, A. (1999). The Origins of the Term Mentor. *History of Education Society Bulletin*, No. 64, November 1999, pp. 313 – 329.

Sprafka, H., & Kranda, A. (2008). Institutionalizing Mentoring in Police Departments. *Police Chief Magazine*, 75(1), 46-49.

Chapter 23

Retention Policies and Strategies

Why Retention Effectiveness Improves the Organization

If law enforcement agencies are successful in hiring quality officers, then they must have an effective method of retaining them. In recent years, law enforcement agencies nationwide have experienced increasing levels of staff turnover and difficulty recruiting new officers. The current challenge is that officers with the most tenure are beginning to retire. After they do retire agencies are finding that they do not have enough experienced officers to take their place. This has caused the average years of experience of departments to drop greatly and decrease the effectiveness of the police force to serve the public, which is its primary goal. High turnover reduces the overall productivity of a law enforcement agency and can lower quality of police service.

Law enforcement agencies need to identify benchmarks for measuring the severity of problem and the cost of turnover to any agency along with the reasons for the loss of personnel. From this information officers can make informed decisions on how to retain officers and recruit candidates who are more likely to identify and stay within the agency. All law enforcement agencies will have some amount of employee turnover, but not enough research has been done to establish a benchmark of accepted turnover rates. A study done by the Florida Department of Law Enforcement found that an officer had to be employed for approximately 3.5 years before a law enforcement department received return-on-investment for hiring and training the individual. If an officer separates before that time, it is a great loss to the department financially and to the community (Orrick, 2008, p.143).

The Cost of Attrition

What are the costs to a law enforcement agency when they lose officers? One budgeted cost to a law enforcement agency is the cost of recruitment. The cost of hiring a new recruit can be extensive based on all the tests and processes required to hire a new officer. A second cost factor is the selection process for hiring law enforcement officers. Third, the money a law enforcement agency has spent on basic training, in-service training, specialized training, and advanced training on officers that have left becomes a sunk cost. This can include any money allocated for educational incentives used to increase the effectiveness of an officer on the job. A fourth major cost is separation costs, which involve paying officers any separation pay after they leave the organization. These are key reasons for police agencies to retain the officers that they already have, especially if they are performing effectively in their job.

To avoid having to hire and recruit so many new officers, agencies should strive to find a way to retain the officers that they already have. This is a major problem for many agencies today that are losing experienced and effective officers. The limiting factor to an increase of the attrition rate is the national economy. The prolonged recession is reducing the number of jobs available so officers are more inclined to remain in their current jobs. Officers who work together for longer periods of time have more shared experiences and operate in a more cohesive manner. Reducing turnover provides more time and resources for advanced training and developing "depth" within the agency. Studies have shown that officers with advanced training are more effective on the job and tend to make fewer mistakes and have fewer disciplinary actions. In today's work environment the multiple knowledge and skills required of police officers make them valuable employees to both the public and private sector (Orrick, 2008, p. 169).

Key Retention Issues

In addition to the costs, another challenge of hiring new recruits is the lack of qualified candidates for the job. In a study by the U. S. Department of Justice, COPS Office, most agencies surveyed nation-wide have had difficulty in attracting qualified candidates (Orrick, 2008, p. 142). This becomes a significant issue as many law enforce-ment officers are reaching retirement eligibility and the need to hire quality officers only increases. The agency must find recruits that are more likely to stay with the agency and commit to a sufficient period of service. In a study done in North Carolina, the researchers found from the agencies that were surveyed that there are three main reasons that officers give for terminating employment: agency budget restrictions, accepting employment in the private sector, and lateral transfers to other law enforcement agencies (Yearwood, 2003). These are the issues that law enforcement leaders must address when implementing retention strategies within their departments.

Agencies who are losing officers must counteract these problems by developing a good strategy or plan. An agency should consider various strategies to increase retention and apply those most appropriate for the organizational environment. One study found six main factors affecting the retention of officers: annual pay increase non-performance based; education/training benefits; promotions; annual pay increase performance based; recognition; and assigned favorable work shifts (Yearwood, 2004). Another study suggested six slightly different methods to positively address the challenges of retention: pay; schedules; recognition; education/ training; improper socialization; and career/mentoring programs (Hertig, 2001). These are all important factors for law enforcement administrators to review when developing retention strategies. However, a more in-depth understanding of the topic of retention is required.

Due to the increase or potential increase of officers retiring it is important for law enforcement leaders to develop and integrate officer-retention strategies into the management of their organization. The focus of their strategy must be to maximize the factors of effective recruitment and to minimize the factors that increase the turnover rate. Law enforcement leaders just as leaders of any other organization must view every employee as a free agent. These free agents at any given point in time may take their talent and abilities to another organization. Every organization must ask the question, why would a person want to continue serving in our organization? What are the organizational assets that help retain qualified employees, and what are the organizational deficiencies that encourage people to leave? The primary issue of consideration usually is salary and benefits. In his best-selling book *Good to Great*, author Jim Collins articulates the appropriate perspective on developing an effective compensation plan. A law enforcement organization should develop a compensation plan that is competitive with other law enforcement organizations in its region that are similar in size. If a compensation plan is relatively competitive, moderately higher degrees of competitive compensation is not sufficient to motivate an officer in wanting to leave the organization. Collins' research indicated that it's not that compensation is irrelevant; you just have to be basically rational and reasonable. The purpose of a compensation system should not be to get the right behaviors from the wrong people, but to get the right people in the organization and to keep them there (Collins, 2001). The primary reason people do quality and ethical work is not because of compensation, it is because this value is intrinsic and therefore just a part of who they are. Another valuable point that comes out of Collins' research is debunking the old adage that people are your most important resource in an organization. In good-to-great organizational transformations, people are not your most important asset. The right people are (Collins, 2001).

A starting competitive salary is ideal. It is obvious that small law enforcement agencies cannot always compete with large agencies regarding their compensation package. However, a competitive starting salary in addition to desirable benefits and other career opportunities can improve retention.

At a minimum, every law enforcement agency ideally wants to retain a newly hired officer for at least five years. This five-year benchmark is probably the minimum return on investment that an agency should seek. Some government agencies pay step increases top out at three years. I recommend that pay step increases should top out at five years minus longevity pay. A step increase for the first five years is a strategy for retaining officers beyond the three-year service mark.

One major challenge with having pay incentives is the agency's budget limitations or restrictions. An agency's budget restriction is found in several studies as the number one reason for officer's separation after their first three years on the job. One study done in North Carolina found that out of those surveyed 82.3 percent said that they separated from their law enforcement agency due to the agency's budget restrictions. If the agency does not have money to provide pay incentives, better equipment, or training, it can deter officers to other agencies or jobs that are well funded (Yearwood, 2003, p. 21).

A lack of educational and training opportunities are another reason why officers choose to separate from their organization. Officers employed with agencies that do not offer sufficient in-service, specialized, advanced training, and educational incentives perceive there is limited professional growth and opportunities for promotion. Law enforcement agencies have found that ongoing professional development programs increase job satisfaction and officer skills. Officers who work for an organization that does not provide such benefits are encouraged to go elsewhere to find them. Agencies seeking to retain quality officers must increase training that addresses relevant issues such as community policing and crime prevention. Administrators should offer more self-directed learning and training opportunities. Law enforcement agencies should have a minimum standard of 40 hours of in-service training for each officer per year. Additionally, management should send their officers to outside training workshops and seminars to increase their professional development. Agencies that offer tuition reimbursement at colleges and universities are more likely to retain higher quality officers.

One of the most cost-effective strategies a law enforcement agency can use is recognizing good performance. A motivating factor for leaving any organization, including a law enforcement organization, is the lack of recognition for a job well done. Individuals motivated to apply for a law enforcement officer job typically have a desire to make a contribution to the community. If their contributions to the community and the organization are not recognized, it potentially becomes a motivating factor for them to seek job satisfaction in another organization. A law enforcement agency should consider such things as: award ribbons for specific operational performance, letters of commendation, pay incentives, an awards program, or other forms of recognition to increase retention.

All new officers must be effectively socialized into their law enforcement agency. When improper socialization occurs, officers are more likely to separate from the organization. Law enforcement organizations are well established as being insular with a fraternal type spirit (historically a man's job, but of course that has changed). A bonding effect occurs, in theory based on the high amount of contact law enforcement officers must have with the perpetrators of crime and other negative elements of our society. Those that are not a suitable organizational fit quickly recognize it, and are likely made to feel like an outsider by other officers (this is seldom discussed). This lack of enjoyable socialization, which is a key job satisfaction factor in any organization, motivates an employee to seek employment in another organization. With the amount of time spent working in the law enforcement environment, one must perceive they are in a comfortable social environment where they can make and maintain friendships. Mentoring is therefore a strategy that should be used (which is discussed in the previous chapter) to overcome the potential for improper socialization.

The negative aspects of the law enforcement work environment drive officers to go elsewhere for employment. To retain quality officers, agencies must be purposeful to manage the organizational environment while offering incentives and benefits to bring a more positive atmosphere to the work environment. A positive organizational culture is designed to address issues within the workplace, which in turn motivates employees to remain in the organization. In law enforcement agencies, like other organizations, managing the organizational culture is a key issue to keeping officers on the job. Being an officer can be a very stressful and complex job. Law enforcement agency administrators must be purposeful and progressive in developing and implementing strategies to retain the most qualified officers.

Recommendations and Key Points of Retention Policies and Strategies

1. If law enforcement agencies are successful in hiring quality officers, then they must have an effective method of retaining them.
2. High turnover reduces the overall productivity of a law enforcement agency and can lower quality of police service.
3. Officers who work together for longer periods of time have more shared experiences and operate in a more cohesive manner.
4. Reducing turnover provides more time and resources for advanced training and developing "depth" within the agency.
5. Law enforcement leaders just as leaders of any other organization must view every employee as a free agent.
6. Every organization must ask the question, why would a person want to continue serving in our organization?
7. If a compensation plan is relatively competitive, moderately higher degrees of competitive compensation is not sufficient to motivate an officer in wanting to leave the organization.
8. The purpose of a compensation system should not be to get the right behaviors from the wrong people, but to get the right people in the organization, and to keep them there.
9. At a minimum, every law enforcement agency ideally wants to retain a newly hired officer for at least five years.
10. It is recommended that pay step increases should top out at five years minus longevity pay.
11. One major challenge with having pay incentives is the agency's budget limitations or restrictions.
12. A lack of educational and training opportunities are another reason why officers choose to separate from their organization.
13. Officers employed with agencies that do not offer sufficient in-service, specialized, advanced training, and educational incentives perceive there is limited professional growth and opportunities for promotion.
14. One of the most cost-effective strategies a law enforcement agency can use is recognizing good performance.
15. When improper socialization occurs, officers are more likely to separate from the organization.
16. Mentoring is a strategy that should be used to overcome the potential for improper socialization.

References

Collins, J. (2001). *Good to Great.* New York, NY: Harper Collins Publishers Inc.

Hertig, C. (2001, August 1). Recruitment and retention strategies. *Access Control & Security System Solutions.*

Koper, C. (2001, October 1). Hiring and Retention Issues in Police Agencies: Readings on the Determinants of Police Strength, Hiring and Retention of Officers, and the Federal COPS Program. *The Urban Institute.*

Orrick, D. (2008). *Recruitment, Retention, and Turnover of Police Personnel.* Springfield: Charles C. Thomas.

Index